Multi-Power
MICROWAVE MIRACLES

FROM
◉ SANYO

Multi-Power

MICROWAVE MIRACLES

FROM

⊕ SANYO

A Rutledge Book
The Benjamin Company, Inc.
New York, New York

by Hyla O'Connor

ISBN: 0-87502-052-6
Library of Congress Catalog Card Number: 77-72352
Prepared and produced by Rutledge Books, a division of
Arcata Consumer Products Corporation.
Published by The Benjamin Company, Inc.
485 Madison Avenue
New York, New York 10022
Printed in Japan
First printing

All Photographs by Walter Storck Studios, Inc.
Illustrations by Tom Huffman

Contents

MARVEL AT COOKING WITH MICROWAVES

Naturally enough, you're anxious to begin using your new microwave oven. But do take the time to review the material in this section. It's not only interesting and helpful; it will pay off for you in terms of getting the most out of your oven.

Although the way the microwave oven works may seem almost miraculous, the basic principles behind its cooking of food are not difficult to understand.

What Microwave Energy Is

The electrical energy for the microwave works on standard household current 110–120v. In the case of a microwave oven, the electrical energy is converted into electromagnetic energy by means of an electron tube located within the oven. This tube, called a magnetron, converts electrical energy into electromagnetic—or microwave—energy, then sends microwaves directly into the food to be cooked.

How Microwaves Cook Food

Microwaves, transmitted by the magnetron, bounce off the interior sides of the oven and pass through suitable cooking utensils to come in direct contact with the food. These microwaves—or short energy waves—are attracted to molecules of moisture, fat, and sugar in the food; they cause the molecules to rub against each other, and eventually to vibrate rapidly. This in turn sets up friction, and the resulting heat engendered cooks the food.

How the Oven Works

When you cook with a conventional range, food heats and is cooked by means of electricity, gas, or wood. On top of the range, the heat applied to the bottom of the pan cooks the food; when food is placed in an oven, the hot air surrounding the food cooks it.

Not so with the microwave oven. The microwaves travel directly to the food. They do not heat the surrounding air or the recommended dishes in which the food is being cooked. There is also no need to wait for the oven to heat, because the cooking action begins instantly.

Installation and Maintenance of the Oven

Both installation and maintenance are quite simple. To install your oven, *follow manufacturer's directions carefully*. A microwave oven operates on standard household current and does not require an expert to ready it for regular use.

Maintenance requires a few simple cleaning steps. Please *follow your manufacturer's directions*. Since there is little splattering with microwave cooking, you'll find that the buildup of grease or the like is minimal; an occasional wiping is all that is required to keep the oven clean. About the only other maintenance necessary is occasional replacement of the light bulb in the interior of the oven.

Keep the door and door gasket free of food buildup to maintain a tight seal.

Using the Oven

The recipes in this book refer to ten cooking levels: WARM, LOW, DEFROST, BRAISE, SIMMER, BAKE, ROAST, REHEAT, SAUTE, and HIGH. These correspond to the percentages of power level indicated on the oven.

The multi-power settings available on your oven open up the possibility of almost infinite variations in cooking. The power range is from 10% to 100%—with gradations in between all the settings. Each of the basic ten settings corresponds to a cooking process or technique. The chart below gives a good idea of what these processes are and what standard uses they can be put to.

COOKING GUIDE FOR MULTI-POWER SETTINGS

Setting	Power	Uses and Information
WARM	10%	Softening cream cheese; proofing bread dough; keeping dinners warm.
LOW	20%	Softening chocolate; heating breads, rolls, pancakes, and French toast.
DEFROST	30%	Defrosting frozen foods; cooking noodles and rice.
BRAISE	40%	Cooking less-tender cuts of meat in liquid (e. g., pot roast, Swiss steak).
SIMMER	50%	Cooking sauces, stews, and soups.
BAKE	60%	Starting cakes and quick breads (such as biscuits and corn breads).
ROAST	70%	Cooking rump roasts, ham, veal, and lamb; cooking cheese dishes; defrosting large cuts of meat and poultry.
REHEAT	80%	Reheating leftovers.
SAUTE	90%	Quickly frying onions, mushrooms, green peppers.
HIGH ("HI")	100%	Cooking poultry, fish, vegetables, and most casseroles; preheating the browning dish.

These ten settings are not the whole story. As you become accustomed to working with your oven, you may find that you would like more flexibility in determining an exact setting. For example, perhaps you opt for a setting between REHEAT and SAUTE. Set the time as usual, adjust the COOK or CUISINE CONTROL so that "85" is indicated, which means that your oven is operating at 85% of power level — half way between REHEAT and SAUTE.

If you decide on a power level just slightly higher than REHEAT, you can adjust to "81", and the oven would be set to operate at 81% of power level.

Because Multi-Power Cook Control allows you to choose any setting you want, you will be able to cook with great flexibility and precision. You can control results so that the end product suits your taste exactly.

The chart below is a guideline to cooking foods to doneness according to their internal temperature.

TEMPERATURE CONTROL

120°	Fully Cooked Ham
125°	Rare Beef
135°	Medium Beef
140°	Meat Loaf
150°	Reheat Casseroles
155°	Well-Done Beef; Veal, Pork
160°	Reheat Vegetables
165°	Well-Done Lamb
170°	Reheat Beverages
175°	Reheat Potatoes

Utensils and Containers

Glass, china, and pottery utensils are ideal for use in a microwave oven because microwaves pass through them. If any of these have metallic trim or glaze, they should not be used.

If you are unsure about the suitability of a particular utensil, place it in the oven on the HIGH setting for 30 seconds. A container that remains cool is safe to use. If it is warm, don't use it.

Check manufacturer's labels, too. Often a utensil will be labeled "Good for Microwave."

Plastics are safe to use if they are dishwasher safe—but use them only for limited cooking periods or for heating. Do not use plastic for tomato-based foods or foods with a high fat or sugar content.

Plastic cooking pouches can be used provided that: 1) metal ties or twisters are removed first and 2) the pouch is slit so that steam can escape.

Paper is good for short-term cooking and for reheating on low heat. It cannot be foil-lined, and remember that prolonged use may cause it to burn. Waxed paper is suitable for preventing splattering.

Straw and wood can be used for quick warming—for instance, for heating rolls. Longer use could cause cracking.

A *browning dish* must be preheated; it's good for browning foods that have too short a cooking time to brown by themselves (pork chops, for instance).

A *microwave roasting rack* made of plastic is suitable; it allows juices to drain from meat or poultry.

Most *metals* are not suitable for use in the microwave oven because they reflect microwaves and interfere with effective cooking. Exceptions to this rule are listed below. If any metal touches the sides of the oven it can cause arcing (sparks in the oven). Any metal used should be at least one inch from the oven wall; otherwise, arcing will occur and may damage the oven.

Exceptions to the No-Metal Rule:

On large pieces of meat or poultry, strips of aluminum foil can be used to cover areas that are becoming overcooked.

TV dinners can be heated in their shallow aluminum trays. (Metal containers used in the oven should not exceed three-fourths of an inch in depth.) However, TV dinners will heat much faster if you "pop" the blocks of food out and arrange them on ordinary dinner plates. (As a general rule of thumb, remember that food mass must always be greater than the amount of metal.)

Remove all metal twisters or foil strips from paper or plastic bags and substitute string; metal or foil may arc and ignite the paper or plastic.

It is very important that only microwave oven meat thermometers be used in the food during microwave cooking. Conventional meat thermometers may be inserted to test the internal temperature after the food has been removed from the oven. If the food has to be cooked further, remove the thermometer before you return the food to the microwave oven.

Do Not Use:

1) Metal twists or ties
2) Pots and pans
3) Baking sheets
4) Dishes with metallic trim or handles

All of these may cause a distorted cooking pattern, arcing, or both.

RECOMMENDED UTENSILS AND CONTAINERS

Item	Good Use	General Notes
China plates and cups (without metal trim)	Heating dinners and coffee	
Pottery plates, mugs, and bowls (unglazed)	Heating dinners, soups, and coffee	
Earthenware (ironstone) plates, bowls, and mugs	Heating dinners, soups, and coffee	If dish has been in refrigerator, may take longer to heat food.
Corelle® Livingware dinnerware	Heating dinners, soups, and coffee	Closed-handle cups should not be used.
Paper plates, cups, and napkins	Heating leftovers, coffee, frankfurters, doughnuts, and rolls	Absorb moisture from baked goods and freshen them.
Soft plastics, such as dessert topping cartons and Tupperware®	Reheating leftovers	Can be used for short reheating periods. Do not use to reheat acid-based foods or those with a high fat or sugar content.
Corningware® casseroles	Cooking main dishes, vegetables, and desserts	
Pyrex® casseroles	Cooking main dishes, vegetables, and desserts	Do not use dishes with metal trim, or arcing may occur.

Item	Good Use	General Notes
TV dinner trays (metal)	Frozen dinners or homemade dinners	Can be no deeper than ³/₄″. However, microwaves will penetrate from the top and the food will receive heat from the top surface only.
Oven film and cooking bags	Cooking roasts or stews	Substitute string for metal twister (twister would cause arcing and bag would melt). Bag itself will not cause tenderizing. Do not use film with foil edges.
Cooking pouches	Cooking meats, vegetables, rice, and other frozen foods	Slit pouch so steam can escape.
Waxed paper	Wrapping corn on the cob; covering casseroles	Microwaves have no effect on wax. However, food temperature may cause some melting. (Wax will not adhere to hot food.)
Plastic wrap	Covering dishes	Puncture to allow steam to escape.
Metal spoons (not silver)	Stirring puddings and sauces	Will not cause arcing as long as there is a quantity of food. Handle may become warm. Do not leave in oven with small amounts of food.
Wooden spoons	Stirring puddings and sauces	Can withstand microwaves for short cooking periods.
Microwave roasting racks	Cooking roasts and chickens	
Browning dishes	Searing, grilling, and frying small meat items; grilling sandwiches	These utensils absorb microwaves and preheat to high temperatures. A special coating on the bottom makes them unique; they brown pieces of meat that otherwise would not brown in a microwave oven.

Important Terms in Microwave Cooking

There are a number of points that are important to remember for successful microwave cooking. Because the oven works so quickly, factors that would not be vital in conventional oven cooking become important. Following are some of the terms and cooking procedures that are integral to this new kind of cooking—along with an explanation of each.

Starting temperature of the food to be heated affects cooking time. Cooking time given in recipes is based on normal storage temperature of ingredients.

For example, milk is usually used right from the refrigerator. Therefore, any recipe that uses milk assumes that the milk will be cold, having been taken directly from the refrigerator.

If you use a particular ingredient that is colder than normal, the cooking time will be a bit longer. Similarly, if an ingredient is warmer than would be usual, the cooking time will decrease to some extent.

In general, the warmer the food or ingredients to start with, the shorter the cooking or heating time. Remember this if you make substitutions in recipes. If you use a frozen ingredient instead of the canned one that the recipe specifies, you'll have to increase the cooking time given in the recipe.

Density refers to the composition of a particular food item. In other words, some foods have a basic structure that consists of molecules that are tightly packed together (a meat roast is one example). When this is the case, it takes microwaves longer to penetrate and cook the food than they would take for a less dense item. A more porous food (such as bread) absorbs microwaves faster and heats through or cooks more quickly.

Volume is a factor that affects cooking time in the microwave oven. Here the word volume refers to the amount of food to be cooked. If you are baking several potatoes, the cooking time will be longer than it would if you were baking just one potato. The same holds true with liquids to be heated: three cups of water will take longer than would just one cup.

If you halve a recipe, cook the food a little more than half the time the recipe calls for. In both cases, keep checking at short intervals until the food is cooked to your taste.

Arrangement of foods within the oven should be taken into consideration. If there are several pieces of similar food, arrange them so that each gets the maximum concentration of microwaves. Potatoes should be arranged in a ring; ears of corn are best placed like spokes of a wheel, from the center of the oven out to the sides. When you reheat a plate of leftovers, denser foods should be placed toward the outer edge of the container. The more porous foods (like bread or rolls) can be positioned in the center of the plate. This way, dense foods get the greatest concentration of microwave energy and there is a more even microwave distribution in all the foods.

Delicate ingredients require a lower setting for proper cooking. Many high-protein foods in the dairy group fall into this category: cheese, eggs, milk, cream, and sour cream. Cooking at a higher heat may cause these foods to toughen, separate, or curdle.

Mayonnaise, kidney beans, and mushrooms also require lower heat. On a higher setting, mayonnaise may separate, kidney beans and mushrooms may "pop."

All of the foods referred to above are penetrated quickly by microwaves and are easily overcooked. Using a lower setting guards against overcooking.

Container size and shape specified in recipes should be followed for best results.

If you vary the size or shape of the container, the cooking time may vary. A tall, narrow container will increase cooking time, just as a shallow, broad container will reduce it.

The containers specified in the recipes have been chosen for a reason. You will find that recipes for puddings and sauces call for containers that are larger than the quantity of liquid being cooked to prevent boilovers. Cake recipes call for round utensils for more even cooking. This is important to ensure good texture in a cake.

Coverings suitable for use in the microwave oven include glass covers, plastic wrap, waxed paper, and glass plates and saucers. Covers are useful because they trap steam and therefore speed cooking time. Furthermore, they seal in natural moisture, preventing foods from drying out as well as preserving nutrients.

Remove any covering away from hands and face to prevent steam burns.

Stirring is necessary for some foods. Because microwaves cook the outside edges of food first, the center portion sometimes needs redistribution for even cooking. This is true of puddings; the redistribution is accomplished simply by stirring. Always stir from the outside in, so that heat is equalized and uncooked portions flow toward the outside edges.

This technique is similar to the top-to-bottom stirring you're accustomed to doing on a range burner. In the microwave oven, however, you need stir only occasionally.

Browning usually takes place naturally. After ten minutes or so, meats and poultry brown. For individual pieces of meat that cook in a shorter period of time (such as hamburgers, pork chops, or steak), use a special microwave browning dish.

If you prefer, you can create a browned look by brushing on a gravy mix or bottled flavor enhancer after the meat is cooked.

Cookies, cakes, and breads do not brown well in the oven. When dark-colored ingredients (such as chocolate or spices) are part of the recipe, the lack of browning is not apparent. Other times, glazes or frostings can be used.

Turning foods over is sometimes necessary. In the case of large, dense foods (e.g., roasts), turning the food over will help to cook it evenly. Generally it is not necessary to rotate the food container. Chicken pieces, pork chops, and other meats with bones should be placed so that the bony part faces the center, the thick part faces the outside. This aids in even cooking.

Standing time is important to microwave cooking. The standing time specified in the recipes is really a part of the cooking time, in that food continues to cook after it is removed from the oven. The more dense the food, the longer the standing time. In addition to finishing the cooking process, standing time helps retain natural juices and makes carving easier.

The recipes in this book all take standing time into account and specify the correct amount of time to allow. With your own recipes, some experimentation may be necessary to gauge proper standing time. As a guideline, use the standing time specified in a similar recipe here.

Meal planning should not pose a problem. Keep in mind that foods that need to be cooked longest should be cooked first. The main dish (such as a roast or a casserole) should be cooked first, then the vegetables and bread cooked or heated. Desserts can be made in the morning—unless they are to be served hot.

Defrosting with Microwaves

One of the most useful functions the microwave oven can perform is defrosting frozen foods. The oven will defrost the food completely without cooking it. The food is then ready to be cooked according to a given recipe.

When you refer to the chart below, please be sure to check the "Notes" for the food you are defrosting. All foods are placed in the oven in their original packages, and are defrosted on the DEFROST setting—*except* when the "Notes" column specifies otherwise.

Food	Minutes per pound	Notes	Total Standing Time (in minutes)
BEEF			
Pot Roast	4–5	Turn once	10
Rump Roast			
3–4 lb.	5–6	Turn once	30
6–7 lb.		Use ROAST setting Turn twice	45
Sirloin Tip Roast	5–7	Turn once	30
Rib Roast, Rolled			
3–4 lb.	6–8	Turn once	30
6–7 lb.		Use ROAST setting Turn twice	45
Rib Roast, Standing	5–6	Turn twice	45
Ground Beef	5–6	Frozen in flat square Turn once	5
Hamburger Patty (4 oz.)	1	Use a glass plate	2
Round Steak	4–5	Turn once	5–10
Flank Steak	4–5	Turn once	5
Sirloin Steak			
(½ inch thick)	5	Turn once	5
Rib Eye Steak	3–4	Turn once	5
Corned Beef	4–5	Turn once	10
Liver (sliced)	5–7	Separate slices Rinse in cold water	5
LAMB OR PORK			
Lamb or Pork Roast	4–5	Turn once	20
Lamb or Pork Chops	4–6	Separate chops then cook 1 more minute per lb.	5
Spareribs	5–7		10

Food	Minutes per pound	Notes	Total Standing Time (in minutes)
VEAL			
Veal roast			
3–4 lb.	5–7	Turn once	20
6–7 lb.		Use ROAST setting Turn twice	
Sliced veal	4–6	Turn slices and separate	10
POULTRY—use original wrapping without metal clips			
Chicken (whole)	6–8	Turn once. Immerse in cold water during standing time	10
Chicken (cut up)	5–6	Turn every 5 minutes. Separate pieces. Continue 3–5 more minutes	10
Turkey (whole)			
8–12 lb.	3–5	Over 8 lb., use ROAST setting. Place breast up to	30
12–16 lb.		start. Turn and let stand	45
16–20 lb.		halfway through defrosting time. Return to oven for remainder of defrosting time. Immerse in cold water	60
Turkey (breast)	4–5	Over 4 lb., use ROAST setting. Let stand 10 min. halfway through defrosting time. Immerse in cold water	10
Turkey (pieces)	5–6	Turn every 5 minutes. Separate pieces. Continue 3–5 more minutes	10
Duckling (whole/4–5 lb.)	4-5	Use ROAST setting. Let stand 10 min. halfway through defrosting time. Immerse in cold water	10
Rock Cornish Game Hen	7–9	Turn once. Immerse in cold water	10

Food	Minutes per pound	Notes	Total Standing Time (in minutes)
FISH/SEAFOOD			
Frozen Fillets	6–8	Use original package. Separate fillets for last half of defrosting time. Rinse in cold water	5
Whole Fish	3–5	Turn once	5
Shrimp or Scallops	5–6	Use LOW setting. Separate pieces for last half of defrosting time	5
Lobster Tail	6–8	Use LOW setting. Rinse in cold water	5
BREADS/PASTRIES/FRUITS			
Loaf of Bread (sliced)	1–3	Use original package	5
Dinner Rolls (1 dozen)	1–3	Use original package	5
Buns (½ doz.)	1–3		1–2
Fruit Pie (9″ baked)	9–12	Use glass pie plate	10
Cake (1 lb.)	2–3		5
Fruit	2–3	Use covered casserole Defrost on HIGH	5

Meat

Meat is usually the main dish. Large cuts of meat cook much more quickly in the microwave than in a conventional oven, so that it's possible to enjoy them even when time is at a premium.

To retain the juices, do not salt the meat before or during the cooking period. The following chart assumes that meat is fresh or thoroughly defrosted. For defrosting information, see page xii.

Before You Start:

1) Place the meat, fat side down, on a plastic microwave roasting rack, or on an inverted saucer in a glass baking dish.

2) Set the microwave on the "First Setting" indicated on the roasting chart below for half of the total cooking time.

3) Turn the meat fat side up. (Larger—7 pounds or more—should be turned 3 times during the cooking period.)

4a) *If you are cooking by time,* set the microwave on the "Second Setting" for the remainder of cooking time.

4b) *If you are using temperature control,* plug the temperature sensor into its receptacle inside the oven cavity and insert the probe securely into the center of the meat. Set the temperature control panel to the desired degree of doneness, the microwave on the "Second Setting" indicated on the chart below. The oven will turn off when the internal temperature is reached.

5) Let the meat stand, covered with foil, about 10 minutes before you carve or serve it. The internal temperature will rise about 15° during this standing time and the meat will continue to cook to the final degree of doneness you have chosen.

MEAT ROASTING CHART

Meat Cut	First Setting	Second Setting	Cooking Time (Minutes per pound)	Doneness (Temperature when meat comes from oven)
BEEF				
Pot Roast	SIMMER	BRAISE	well-done: 15–16	155° F
Rump Roast	ROAST	SIMMER	rare: 11–12	125° F
			medium: 13–14	135° F
			well-done: 15–16	155° F
Sirloin Tip Roast	HIGH	ROAST	rare: 8–9	125° F
			medium: 10–11	135° F
			well-done: 12–13	155° F
Rib Roast, Rolled	HIGH	ROAST	rare: 8–9	125° F
			medium: 10–11	135° F
			well-done: 12–13	155° F
Rib Roast, Standing	HIGH	ROAST	rare: 7–8	125° F
			medium: 9–10	135° F
			well-done: 11–12	155° F
Meat Loaf	ROAST	ROAST	well-done: 25–30	155° F
LAMB OR PORK				
Lamb Roast	ROAST	ROAST	well-done: 10–11	160° F
Pork Roast	HIGH	ROAST	well-done: 10–11	155° F
Ham (boneless):				
ready to eat or canned	ROAST	ROAST	(heated) 10–12	120° F
Ham (bone in)	ROAST	ROAST	(heated) 9–11	120° F
VEAL				
Veal Roast	ROAST	SIMMER	well-done: 20–22	155° F

Poultry

Poultry is an all-around favorite in most families. The chart below gives guidelines for cooking whole birds in the microwave oven. (The chart assumes that poultry is fresh or completely defrosted; see page xii for defrosting chart.)

Before You Start:

1) Wash the bird and set aside the giblets. Sprinkle inside of the cavity with salt. If desired, fill the cavity and neck opening with stuffing (stuffing the bird will not affect the cooking time). Fasten the openings with *wooden* picks; tie the legs together and tie the wings to the body with string.

2) Place the bird, breast side down, on a microwave roasting rack in a baking dish. Brush the bird with melted butter or margarine.

3) Cook, uncovered, for the first half of the cooking time, using the "First Setting" indicated on the chart.

4) Turn the bird breast side up.

5) Cook, uncovered, using the "Second Setting" indicated on the chart for the remaining cooking time or until the meat thermometer registers 175° (temperature will increase to 195° during standing time).

6) If you notice some areas (such as wing tips or legs) cooking more rapidly than others, you can cover the areas with small pieces of foil. The foil will slow down the cooking in that area.

7) Let the bird stand, covered with foil, 10 minutes. (Larger birds will require longer standing time.)

POULTRY ROASTING CHART

Meat Cut	First Setting	Second Setting	Cooking Time (Minutes per pound)
Chicken (whole)	HIGH	HIGH	8–9
Chicken (cut up)	HIGH	HIGH	8–9
Turkey (whole)	HIGH	ROAST	8–9
Turkey (breast)	ROAST	ROAST	11–12
Turkey (pieces)	ROAST	ROAST	15–16
Duckling (whole)	ROAST	ROAST	10–11
Rock Cornish Game Hen	HIGH	HIGH	9–10

Cakes

Follow the guidelines below, and you'll have successful results every time. You'll also find very helpful information in the *Guidelines for Adapting Your Own Recipes* (under Cakes).

1) No need to use cake flour; all-purpose flour works very well.

2) It's not necessary to sift the flour.

3) Reduce the leavening used (whether baking powder or baking soda) by one-fourth to one-third.

4) For a cake with a heavy batter, insert a glass in the center of the batter in the baking dish. This will create a tube cake and will ensure more even cooking.

To adapt your own recipes, choose a similar recipe in this book and use it as a guide.

Reheating with Microwaves

The microwave oven will reheat a variety of foods to serving temperature without cooking them further. Thus there is no toughening or drying out, and foods retain fresh-cooked flavor and appeal. Check the *Chart of Recommended Utensils and Containers* on page vii for a list of suitable containers and covers to use when reheating foods.

    Here are suggested guidelines for reheating.

Food	Quantity	Time at REHEAT Setting
MEATS AND POULTRY		
Sliced Turkey, Ham, Pork, or Beef	2 ounces	1–1½ minutes
Hamburger	1 patty	1–1¼ minutes
Chicken	1 piece	1–2 minutes
MAIN DISHES/CASSEROLES		
Spaghetti with Sauce	1 cup serving	3–4 minutes
Chili Con Carne	1 cup serving	3–4 minutes
Meat-Vegetable/Noodle Casseroles	1 cup serving	3–4 minutes
Dinner: Meat, Potato, Vegetables	1 dinner plate serving	2½–3 minutes
VEGETABLES/SIDE DISHES		
Rice or Noodles	1 cup serving	2–3 minutes
Mashed Potatoes	1 cup serving	2–3 minutes
Cooked Vegetables	½ cup serving	1½–2 minutes
BREADS AND PASTRIES		
Bread Slice	1 slice	10–15 seconds
Doughnuts/Sweet Rolls	1	15–20 seconds
Dinner Rolls/Muffins/Biscuits	1	10–20 seconds
Cake	1 slice	20–30 seconds
Pie	1 slice	30–40 seconds

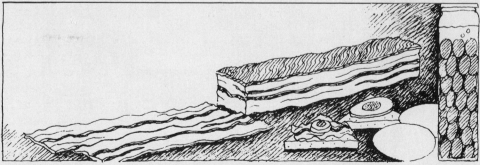

Adapting Recipes

To get the most out of your microwave oven, your own favorite recipes can be adapted for microwave cooking.

First, find a recipe in this book that's similar to the recipe you'd like to try. Use the microwave recipe for guidelines on cooking time, container size, power setting, and ingredients. Or cook the dish for one-fourth of the conventional cooking time, then add time (in short segments) until the food is cooked to your liking.

This chart will give you a general idea of how to proceed.

GUIDELINES FOR ADAPTING YOUR OWN RECIPES

Foods	Suggested Setting(s)	General Information
Appetizers and Sandwiches	HIGH and ROAST	Use already-toasted bread. Do not assemble canapes until ready to microwave, or crackers and toast will become soggy. Appetizers with crust do not microwave well (pastry stays pale). Dips heat well, stay smooth, and do not scorch.
Rib, Leg of Lamb, Pork Loin Roasts	ROAST	Meat will brown somewhat but not as much as in a conventional oven. Standing time is especially important, as some cooking occurs after roast is removed from the oven.
Chuck and Round Roasts	BRAISE	Less browning than in a conventional oven. The LOW setting allows tough meat fibers to become tender; the longer the cooking time, the more tender the meat becomes. If you wish, you can pre-brown the roast on top of a conventional range. Cover; add liquid.

Foods	Suggested Setting(s)	General Information
Stewing Beef	BRAISE	Depending on cut and size of pieces, will cook at different rates. Acceptable results in minimum time, but the longer the cooking time, the more tender the meat will be. Use less liquid than you would in a conventional recipe.
Bacon, Steak, Chops	HIGH	Bacon will brown because of its high fat content. Use browning dish for steaks and chops.
Meat Loaf and Ham	ROAST	Browning approximately the same as with conventional cooking. Cured meats contain sugar, concentrated in spots, and may overcook if not watched carefully.
Poultry and Game Birds	HIGH and ROAST	Poultry becomes very tender. Skin will be soft except for more fatty birds, such as ducks. Final color is golden brown rather than crispy brown.
Fish and Seafood	HIGH	Fish will retain more moisture than in conventional cooking. Remains tender; cooking in a sauce ensures excellent results.

Foods	Suggested Setting(s)	General Information
Eggs and Custard	ROAST	Do not cook eggs in the shell (they will explode). Scrambled eggs are light and tender. Fried eggs can be cooked in browning dish. Do not cook puffy omelets. Custard requires curdling.
Cheese	ROAST	Cheese should be melted or cooked at a ROAST setting. Cheese sauce and fondue should be stirred occasionally.
Rice and Pastas	DEFROST	Microwave saves some time, but not a great deal. Add 1 tablespoon of salad oil to boiling water to prevent boilovers. Use large dish.
Fruits and Vegetables	HIGH	Tender-crisp results. Very little additional water needed, with maximum amount of natural moisture retained. No scorching.

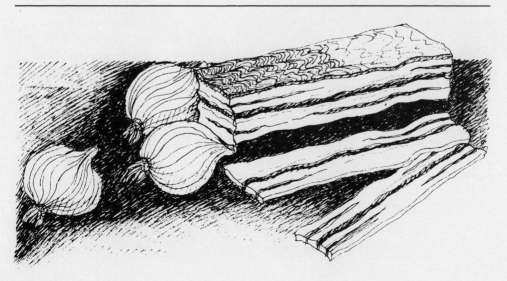

Foods	Suggested Setting(s)	General Information
Cakes, Quick Breads, Yeast Breads, Cookies	BAKE	These do not form a crust, are lighter than conventionally baked goods. Top of cakes may be wet-looking after cooking. Do not overcook to remove the moist appearance, or product will toughen. When you adapt a conventional recipe, reduce baking powder and soda by a fourth or a third. Baked products will be pale (except chocolate or spice mixtures). Angel food and chiffon cakes do not bake well in the microwave. Microwave works best for bar cookies that need no browning and should remain soft.
Frostings and Candies	ROAST	These sugar mixtures cook very quickly, with excellent results. Use buttered large heat-proof bowl. Very little stirring required. Check temperature with candy thermometer after cooking periods (and after removal from oven).
Sauces and Fillings (thickened by flour or cornstarch)	HIGH	Microwave gives excellent results. Blend flour or cornstarch well before cooking. Stir halfway through cooking period in order to prevent lumping. Use slightly less liquid than in conventional recipes. Will not scorch.

Foods	Suggested Setting(s)	General Information
Pies	HIGH and ROAST	Crust becomes flaky but does not brown. Cook crust first before adding filling. Excellent results are achieved by starting in the microwave and finishing in a conventional oven.
Frozen Foods	REHEAT, ROAST, and SIMMER	Reheat in microwave. Cover foods to retain moisture. Use a container that conforms to the shape of the frozen food.

The Miracle of Cooking with Microwaves

Microwave cooking, indeed miraculous, now is even more so. Your multi-power microwave oven offers a versatility never before possible in cooking. Its temperature controls are as sensitive to your fingertips as were the gas and electric oven dials of yesterday. For the first time, *you* control the cooking process and you can vary it according to your own requirements.

Before you use your new oven—and to ensure that you get the most out of it —please take the time to read these few pages and the special section at the front of the book. Once you're familiar with the general guidelines and have found how each of the power settings can serve you, you can experiment with your own ideas and recipes.

What Are the Advantages of Microwave Cooking?

Speed, of course, is the most obvious advantage that most people immediately associate with microwave cooking. The microwave oven cuts cooking time drastically—foods cook in as little as ¼ the time required in a conventional oven. Translated into specific examples, this means that you can bake a potato in 5 minutes, cook a meat loaf in just 17 minutes, have a casserole on the table in a matter of minutes, or serve forth a baked custard in only 8 minutes.

Because the microwave is so fast, the *natural good flavor* of foods is retained. Since there is little moisture loss, important vitamins, minerals, and other nutrients are retained.

Add to these the advantage of *convenience.* You can warm desserts or rolls on a plate, warm coffee in a cup, or heat soup right in the bowl. A meal can be heated on a dinner plate. Leftovers can go right from the refrigerator to the oven if they are in glass dishes. Cooking utensils are much easier to clean after use in a microwave oven, and you often use fewer of them. Sometimes your "utensils" are paper, and you just throw them away after using them. How's that for cutting down on cleanup chores!

Comfort ranks high on the list of microwave advantages, too. The entire kitchen isn't heated when you're "cooking microwave-fashion," so your oven is a special boon in hot weather.

Your microwave oven is an *energy saver;* it both heats up and cools off almost instantly. There's no energy wasted either way.

To top all of this off, the microwave oven is incredibly *easy to use.* It can make true do-it-yourselfers out of the rest of the family, since not only is it easy to use, but the "miracle" aspects of its quick cooking always prove intriguing. It's fun to use—and appetites can be swiftly satisfied.

How a Microwave Oven Works

First, it's basic to understand what a microwave is. Essentially, as the name suggests, a microwave is a short wave of energy. A tube in the microwave oven—

called a magnetron—converts electrical energy into microwave energy. These short energy waves penetrate food, setting the food molecules in motion and causing friction within the food. Friction generates heat, and thus the food is cooked.

Cooking Techniques

Multi-power microwave oven cooking brings a tremendous degree of flexibility to microwave cooking. You can choose the speed at which foods cook; with time and practice, you will find this oven as convenient as your electric or gas oven is right now.

The Cook Control panel on your oven is labeled from WARM to HIGH, each setting corresponding to a 10% increase in power, with infinite settings in between. Each setting has its specific purposes (see chart on insert page iv). As you experiment with the oven, you will soon discover which of the settings (or any of the points in between) work best for you and your recipes.

Cooking Utensils

First point to remember: *do not* use metal utensils in your microwave oven. There are a few exceptions, but that's the usual rule. The following general guidelines should be followed (check insert pages at front of book for more details).

Glass utensils, such as ovenproof glass or oven baking dishes, are excellent for use in the microwave oven. Dishes will remain cool unless the cooking time is prolonged (this may cause the hot food to heat the cooking dish). Glass, sturdy china, and pottery serving dishes can be used safely as long as they do not have silver, gold, or other metal trim.

Manufacturers produce new items all the time for use in the microwave oven; check labels for information about suitability.

Fine china is not ovenproof. Do not use it at all if it has a metal signature on the bottom, or any other metal trim.

If you are uncertain about the suitability of any glass, pottery, or china utensil, test it by placing the empty dish in the oven on HIGH for 30 seconds. If the dish feels warm when it is taken from the oven, do not use it for cooking or heating.

Plastic containers that are dishwasher safe can be used for cooking or heating. However, these containers can develop burn spots if you heat foods that have a high acid, sugar, or fat content. Foam cups and dishes, loosely covered, can be used for individual servings. For prolonged heating, warm the food in the plastic container long enough to loosen it, then remove and place it in a glass casserole or bowl to finish heating. Melamine plastics are not safe for the microwave oven; Melmas plastics are, but they may discolor.

Plastic wrap can be used on top of dishes or casseroles as a tight covering, but it should first be pierced or slit. This will allow the release of steam as the food cooks, and thus prevent steam burns on hands when the covering is removed.

Plastic cooking pouches or boil-in-bags can be used, but they too should be slit before they are placed in the oven. (Make sure that any metal tie, twister, or foil strip is removed first.)

Paper products of all kinds can be used. Paper cups for hot drinks, paper plates and paper napkins or towels are all invaluable aids in successful micro-wave cooking. Waxed paper forms a good covering over dishes or bowls; it keeps splattering down.

Sample Menus to Get You Started

You can prepare a whole meal in your microwave oven. Here is a menu for a quick and easy family dinner.

Spring Pea Soup (page 28)
Beef Goulash (page 34)   Heated Hard Rolls
Tossed Green Salad
Apple Betty (page 150)   Instant Coffee (page 127)

Meal Plan: Make the Apple Betty first, then let it stand while you cook the goulash. While that cooks, prepare the salad. Now make the soup, letting the goulash stand. The hard rolls heat in a matter of seconds. Make coffee and—dinner is served.

Now try a menu for guests. For a special dinner, serve:

Cheddar Cheese Canapés (page 14)   Cocktail Shrimp (page 19) with Dip
Cream Sudanese (page 22)
Cordon Bleu Veal (page 54)   Green Beans Piquant (page 96)
Cauliflower and Tomatoes (page 105)
Lettuce Wedges with Russian Dressing
Vanilla Mousse with Strawberry Sauce (page 146)   Demitasse

Meal Plan: Cook the shrimp and make the dessert in the morning so that they have time to chill. Prepare the veal and let it stand until you are ready to cook it. Prepare the lettuce and its dressing before the guests arrive. Make the Cheddar Cheese Canapés just before you serve them. Prepare the vegetables and let them stand for the few minutes that it takes to cook the veal. Have the soup prepared and ready to cook once the veal is done. The coffee of course takes only minutes.

With the microwave oven, a Sunday brunch can be as much fun for the hostess as for her guests. Offer your friends

Mulled Pineapple Juice (page 124)
Eggs Benedict (page 82)   Sautéed Mushrooms (page 106)
Sticky Buns (page 138)   Café au Lait (page 127)

Meal Plan: Make the Sticky Buns first, then prepare and serve the pineapple juice. While your guests are sipping juice, you can cook the Eggs Benedict and the mushrooms. Coffee is made in moments.

As you become more familiar with your microwave oven, you'll find yourself organizing and serving many microwave meals, of excellent variety and delectable taste, from plans like these. Note that the preparation sequence differs from the sequence in which courses are served. This is true of meals prepared with a conventional range, so it shouldn't really require adjustment on your part. (See page ix for more information about meal planning in general.)

A Final Word

The first time you cook any food, plan on it being an experiment. Cooking times can vary slightly depending on your home's electrical voltage, the starting temperature of the ingredients, and the amount of food. Use the minimum recommended cooking time, then adjust with 30-second additional heatings, if necessary. Take care of your microwave oven, always check with the manufacturer's instructions and/or booklet, and your microwave oven will serve you long and well.

USER INSTRUCTIONS

PRECAUTIONS TO AVOID POSSIBLE EXPOSURE TO EXCESSIVE MICROWAVE ENERGY

(a) DO NOT ATTEMPT to operate this oven with the door open since open-door operation can result in harmful exposure to microwave energy. It is important not to defeat or tamper with the safety interlocks.

(b) DO NOT PLACE any object between the oven front face and the door or allow soil or cleaner residue to accumulate on sealing surfaces.

(c) DO NOT OPERATE the oven if it is damaged. It is particularly important that the oven door closes properly and that there is no damage to the:
(1) DOOR (bent)
(2) HINGES AND LATCHES (broken or loosened)
(3) DOOR SEALS AND SEALING SURFACES.

(d) THE OVEN SHOULD NOT BE ADJUSTED OR REPAIRED BY ANYONE EXCEPT PROPERLY QUALIFIED SERVICE PERSONNEL.

Appetizers

Appetizers, prepared days or weeks before and frozen, can be served piping hot in minutes with the aid of the microwave oven. Canapés with a bread or cracker base should be assembled just before warming to prevent sogginess. Place canapés on a tray or platter with an underliner of paper towels or paper napkins to absorb any moisture. If you are heating a large number of canapés, discard the paper underliner and place heated canapés on a serving plate—not merely for the sake of attractive service but also to keep the canapés from resting on a damp surface.

The microwave oven is ideal for dips and dunks of all kinds—they can be prepared long in advance, placed in serving bowls, and heated in the serving dish with no fuss or bother.

Sweet and Sour Hot Dogs   6 to 8 servings

2 tablespoons prepared mustard   ½ pound frankfurters
¼ cup grape jelly   1 teaspoon butter or margarine, melted

1. Combine mustard and jelly in a 1-cup measuring cup.
2. Cook, covered with plastic wrap, on BAKE for 3 minutes.
3. Cut each frankfurter diagonally in 9 to 10 slices. Put in a 1-quart baking dish with butter.
4. Cook, covered, on HIGH for 2 minutes.
5. Pour grape jelly sauce over frankfurters. Cook, covered, on HIGH for 4 minutes.
6. Let stand 2 minutes.
7. Serve hot; use toothpicks to pick up individual slices.

Cocktail Wieners   6 to 8 servings

¼ cup minced onion   2 tablespoons brown sugar
2 teaspoons butter   ½ teaspoon salt
½ cup catsup   ½ teaspoon dry mustard
1 tablespoon vinegar   ½ teaspoon paprika
½ teaspoon Worcestershire sauce   2 to 3 dozen cocktail wieners

1. Combine onion and butter in a 1- to 1½-quart casserole.
2. Cook, covered, on SAUTE for 3 minutes, or until onion is soft.
3. Add ¼ cup water and stir in remaining ingredients except cocktail wieners.
4. Cook, covered, on HIGH for 2½ minutes, or until sauce is bubbly.
5. Stir in cocktail wieners.
6. Cook, covered, on HIGH for 4 minutes, or until wieners are hot.
7. Let stand, covered, for 2 minutes.
8. Serve warm; use toothpicks to spear individual wieners.

Cheddar Cheese Canapés   24 canapés

¼ cup grated Cheddar cheese   ⅛ teaspoon hot-pepper sauce
2 tablespoons cream   1 tablespoon sesame seeds
1 tablespoon grated Parmesan cheese   24 rounds of toast or crisp crackers
⅛ teaspoon Worcestershire sauce   Chopped parsley

1. Combine Cheddar cheese, cream, Parmesan cheese, Worcestershire, hot-pepper sauce, and sesame seeds. Blend with an electric mixer until smooth.
2. Spread 1 teaspoon of the mixture on each of the toast rounds or crackers.
3. Arrange on a platter lined with paper towels.
4. Cook on ROAST for 30 seconds, or just until mixture is warm and cheese is melted.
5. Garnish with parsley; serve warm.

Rumaki

about 36 appetizers

1 can (8 ounces) water chestnuts   **12 slices bacon**

1. Drain water chestnuts and cut into thirds.
2. Cut bacon slices into thirds. Place a piece of water chestnut on a piece of bacon and roll bacon around it. Secure with a toothpick. Roll remaining water chestnuts and bacon.
3. Place ten at one time on a plate covered with paper towels. Cover top with a paper towel. Cook on HIGH for 2 minutes. Turn over. Cook on HIGH for 2 more minutes.
4. Let stand 1 minute before serving.

Mushroom-Egg Canapes

18 canapes

2 tablespoons butter or margarine   **1 tablespoon chopped parsley**
1 tablespoon finely minced onion   **½ teaspoon salt**
½ cup finely chopped mushrooms   **18 toast rounds or crackers**
2 hard-cooked eggs, finely chopped   **¼ cup grated Cheddar cheese**

1. Put butter, onion, and mushrooms in a small mixing bowl. Cook, uncovered on SAUTE for 3 minutes, or just until mushrooms are soft.
2. Stir in eggs, parsley, and salt.
3. Spread 1 rounded teaspoon of mixture on each toast round. Sprinkle with grated Cheddar cheese.
4. Arrange on a tray lined with paper towels.
5. Cook on REHEAT for 30 seconds, or just long enough to melt the cheese.
6. Serve warm.

Shrimp Dip

2 cups

1 can (10½ ounces) cream of shrimp   **1 teaspoon lemon juice**
soup, undiluted   **Dash of paprika**
1 package (8 ounces) cream cheese,   **Dash of garlic powder**
softened

1. Pour soup into a small mixing bowl.
2. Cook, covered, on BAKE for 3 minutes, or until hot. Stir well.
3. Beat in cream cheese, lemon juice, paprika, and garlic powder. Cook on BAKE for 1½ minutes.
4. Keep warm over a candle warmer. Serve as a dip with crisp vegetables.

FOLLOWING PAGES: Left, *Bean Dip, page 19; Cocktail Wieners, page 14; Hot Mexican Cheese Dip, page 20;* right, *Cocktail Shrimp, page 19; Meatball Appetizers, page 20; Shrimp Dip, page 15.*

Crab Supremes

16 to 18 canapés

1 can (6½ to 7 ounces) crab meat
½ cup finely minced celery
2 teaspoons prepared mustard
4 teaspoons chopped sweet
   pickle relish

½ cup mayonnaise
Crisp crackers or toast rounds

1. Drain crab meat. Place in a 1-quart bowl and flake with a fork. Add celery, mustard, pickle relish, and mayonnaise. Mix well.
2. Spread mixture on crackers or toast rounds. Place 8 at a time on a plate lined with a paper towel.
3. Cook on HIGH for 30 seconds to 1 minute, or until piping hot.

Shrimp Olive Dip

about 2½ cups

1 can (10½ ounces) cream of shrimp
   soup, undiluted
1 package (8 ounces) cream cheese,
   cut into chunks
1 can (8 ounces) chopped ripe olives,
   drained

2 tablespoons lemon juice
1 teaspoon Worcestershire sauce
¾ teaspoon curry powder
   (optional)

1. Combine soup and cream cheese in a 1-quart casserole.
2. Cook, covered, on BAKE for 3 minutes.
3. Remove and stir until cheese is well blended. Stir in remaining ingredients.
4. Cook, covered, on BAKE for 2 to 3 minutes, or until piping hot.
5. Place over a candle warmer to keep hot and serve as a dip with corn chips or potato chips.

Stuffed Mushrooms

makes 8 to 10

8 to 10 medium mushrooms
2 tablespoons minced onion
3 tablespoons butter or margarine

¼ cup dry bread crumbs
¼ teaspoon hot-pepper sauce
2 tablespoons sherry

1. Wipe mushrooms with a damp paper towel. Carefully twist off stems from mushroom caps, leaving caps intact. Chop stems very fine. Place in a small mixing bowl with onion and butter. Cook, uncovered, at HIGH for 3 to 4 minutes, or until onion is tender.
2. Combine mushroom mixture with bread crumbs, hot-pepper sauce, and sherry and mix well. Fill mushroom caps with this stuffing. Place filled mushrooms in an 8-inch baking dish.
3. Cook, covered, on BAKE for 4 minutes, or until mushrooms are piping hot.

Tantalizer Spread

¾ cup

3 strips bacon
1 small tomato, peeled and quartered
1 teaspoon prepared mustard
1 package (3 ounces) cream cheese,
cut into cubes

¼ teaspoon celery salt
½ cup blanched almonds

1. Place paper towels in bottom of an 8-inch square dish. Place bacon strips on towels. Cover loosely with another paper towel.
2. Cook on HIGH for 3½ minutes, or until bacon is very crisp.
3. Put tomato, mustard, cream cheese, and celery salt in blender container. Cover and process until mixture is smooth. Add almonds and bacon and process only until almonds are chopped.
4. Serve with an assortment of crackers.

Bean Dip

3 cups

1 can (1 pound) baked or kidney
beans
1 jar (8 ounces) pasteurized process
cheese spread

¼ cup chili sauce
1 teaspoon chili powder
Dash of hot-pepper sauce

1. Pour beans into a 1½-quart casserole. Mash beans with a fork. Add remaining ingredients and blend well.
2. Cook, covered, on BAKE for 2 to 3 minutes. Stir well.
3. Cook, covered, on SIMMER for 2 to 3 minutes, or until piping hot.
4. Keep hot on a heated tray or a candle warmer.

Cocktail Shrimp

2 to 3 servings

½ pound medium raw shrimp
¼ cup butter or margarine

1 clove garlic, minced
3 tablespoons dry white wine

1. Remove shells and veins from shrimp. Rinse in cold water.
2. Place butter, garlic, and white wine in an 8-inch baking dish or shallow casserole.
3. Cook on HIGH for 2 minutes.
4. Stir mixture and place shrimp in dish. Cover loosely with a piece of waxed paper.
5. Cook on HIGH for 4 minutes, or until shrimp are pink in color and just tender. Do not overcook or shrimp will be tough.
6. Pour shrimp and sauce into a small bowl. Season with salt.
7. Chill and serve as an appetizer with desired dunking sauce.

Hot Mexican Cheese Dip

2½ cups

1 pound process American cheese, **1 can (10 ounces) green chilies and**
grated **tomatoes**

1. Combine cheese and chilies in a 1½-quart casserole.
2. Cook, covered, on REHEAT for 5 minutes. Stir thoroughly.
3. Keep hot on a heated tray or candle warmer, and serve with corn chips or potato chips or with crisp raw vegetables.

Deviled Toasties

30 to 35 canapés

½ pound lean ground round steak **½ teaspoon prepared mustard**
2 tablespoons minced onion **⅛ teaspoon prepared horseradish**
1 teaspoon catsup **1 loaf party rye bread**

1. Combine meat, onion, catsup, mustard, and horseradish. Blend well. Put about 1 teaspoon of the mixture on the top of each little slice of bread.
2. Cook, uncovered, 9 at a time on a paper towel on HIGH for 50 seconds, or to the desired degree of doneness. Remove to serving plate at once.

Meatball Appetizers

about 72

1 pound ground beef **1 cup dry bread crumbs**
½ pound ground pork **1 teaspoon salt**
1 small onion, finely minced **¼ teaspoon pepper**
1 cup milk **¼ teaspoon ground allspice**
1 egg, lightly beaten

1. Combine ingredients in a large mixing bowl and blend well. Form into small balls, about 1 inch in diameter.
2. Arrange half of the meatballs in a single layer in an oblong baking dish.
3. Cook, uncovered, on BAKE for 4 minutes.
4. Place in a chafing dish to keep hot.
5. Cook remaining meatballs.
6. Serve hot with toothpicks and favorite dunking sauce, if desired.

Soups

Soup any time of the day is a snap with the help of the microwave oven. Prepared soups can be heated right in the serving bowls—great for quick service, and never a pot to wash. Soup combinations and simple chowders are fun and easy to make, and a fine way to use up leftovers.

Cream of Mushroom Soup

6 servings

2 cups chopped fresh mushrooms
½ teaspoon onion powder
⅛ teaspoon garlic powder
⅛ teaspoon white pepper
¼ teaspoon salt
2½ cups chicken broth
1 cup heavy cream

1. Combine mushrooms, seasonings, and broth in a 2-quart casserole.
2. Cook on HIGH for 4 minutes, stirring once.
3. Stir in cream.
4. Cook on BAKE for 2 minutes, or until piping hot.

Superb Cream of Chicken

3 servings

1 can (10½ ounces) condensed cream
  of chicken soup, undiluted
1 soup can milk
1 pimiento, diced
¼ cup chopped ripe olives
½ teaspoon turmeric

1. Combine all ingredients in a 1-quart ovenproof bowl or measuring cup.
2. Cook on HIGH for 3 to 4 minutes, or until piping hot.

Cream Sudanese

4 servings

1 can (10½ ounces) condensed cream
  of tomato soup, undiluted
1 can (10½ ounces) condensed pea
  soup, undiluted
½ cup heavy cream
3 tablespoons sherry

1. Place both soups and 1½ soup cans of water in a 1½-quart ovenproof bowl. Stir to blend well.
2. Cook on LOW for 2 minutes.
3. Stir in cream and sherry.
4. Cook on BAKE for 2 minutes, or until piping hot.

Egg Drop Soup

4 servings

2 cans (13¾ ounces) chicken broth
1 tablespoon cornstarch
1 can (4 ounces) water chestnuts, diced
2 scallions, chopped, including green
  tops
2 eggs, slightly beaten
Salt to taste

1. Put chicken broth in a 1½-quart casserole or mixing bowl.
2. Cook, covered, on HIGH for 4 minutes.
3. Combine cornstarch with 2 tablespoons water. Stir in hot broth. Stir in water chestnuts and scallions.
4. Cook, covered, on HIGH for 2 minutes, or until mixture is clear and piping hot.
5. Remove and quickly stir in beaten eggs. Taste, and season with salt, if necessary.

Indienne Cream

6 servings

2 cans (10½ ounces each) condensed
   cream of celery soup, undiluted
2 soup cans milk

1 teaspoon curry powder
2 medium apples, peeled, cored, and
   diced

1. Place soup in a 2-quart ovenproof bowl. Stir in milk and curry powder, mixing well.
2. Cook on HIGH for 3 minutes, or until piping hot.
3. Stir in apples. Cook on HIGH for 1 minute.

Potato Parsley Soup

4 servings

3 cups peeled, diced potatoes
¼ cup chopped onion
¼ teaspoon salt
1 can (13¾ ounces) chicken broth

1 small bunch parsley, chopped
2 tablespoons cornstarch
1½ to 2 cups milk

1. Combine potatoes, onion, salt, and broth in a 2-quart casserole. Add parsley.
2. Cook, covered, on HIGH for 14 minutes, or until potatoes are tender.
3. Combine cornstarch with a small amount of cold milk. Stir into potato mixture. Add remaining milk.
4. Cook, uncovered, on HIGH for 3 to 4 minutes, or until mixture comes to a boil and is piping hot. Stir once during cooking time.

Cheese Soup

4 servings

2½ cups beef broth
½ cup chopped onions

½ teaspoon celery powder
1½ cups grated sharp Cheddar cheese

1. In a 2-quart bowl combine beef broth, onion, and celery powder.
2. Cook on HIGH for 3 minutes.
3. Stir in cheese, blending well.
4. Cook on BAKE for 1 minute, or until cheese is melted.
5. Stir well before serving.

Cold Cucumber Soup

4 servings

2 cups chicken broth
3 large cucumbers
½ teaspoon salt

¼ teaspoon white pepper
1 tablespoon grated onion
1 cup light cream

1. Place chicken broth in a 2-quart ovenproof bowl.
2. Peel and dice 2 of the cucumbers and half of the third. Add to the chicken broth along with salt, pepper, and onion.
3. Cook on HIGH for 14 minutes, or until cucumbers soften.
4. Remove from oven and puree in a blender or force through a sieve. Cool.
5. Stir in cream and refrigerate.
6. Just before serving, float several slices of cucumber on top of each serving.

FOLLOWING PAGES: Left, *Cioppino, page 26;* right, *Quebec Green Pea Soup, page 28.*

Turkey Stock

2 quarts

1 turkey carcass from a 10-pound turkey
(approximately)
2 stalks celery with leaves
1 small onion

1 teaspoon salt
½ teaspoon peppercorns
Pinch of mixed herbs

1. Strip all the meat from the turkey carcass. Break up body bones and place with leg and wing bones in a 3- or 4-quart casserole. Add remaining ingredients. Fill casserole a little over half full with water.
2. Cook, uncovered, on HIGH for 45 minutes.
3. Strain and use stock as desired.

Carrot Chowder

5 to 6 servings

4 slices bacon
1 can (1 pound) diced carrots
1 tablespoon grated onion

¼ cup finely diced celery
2 cups chicken broth

1. Cook bacon according to instructions on page 60. Crumble and reserve.
2. Place carrots, including liquid from can, in a 2-quart ovenproof bowl. Add remaining ingredients and stir well.
3. Cook on HIGH for 3 minutes, or until piping hot.
4. Stir in crumbled bacon before serving.

Note: Three hard-cooked eggs peeled and chopped may be added to the chowder along with the bacon if desired.

Cioppino

8 servings

1 large onion, chopped
1 medium green pepper, seeded and
chopped
½ cup thinly sliced celery
3 cloves garlic, minced
3 tablespoons olive oil
1 can (3 pounds 3 ounces) peeled
Italian tomatoes with puree
1 can (8 ounces) tomato sauce
1 teaspoon basil
1 bay leaf

1 teaspoon salt
¼ teaspoon pepper
1 pound firm white fish
1 dozen mussels or littleneck clams
in the shell
1½ cups dry white wine
½ pound whole shrimp, cleaned and
deveined
½ pound scallops
Chopped parsley

1. Combine onion, pepper, celery, garlic, and olive oil in a 4-quart casserole.
2. Cook on SAUTE for about 5 minutes, or until onion is soft.
3. Mash tomatoes with a fork or potato masher so that whole tomatoes are broken up in small pieces. Add tomatoes to casserole. Add tomato sauce, basil, bay leaf, salt, and pepper.
4. Cook, covered, on HIGH for 15 minutes to blend flavors.
5. While sauce is cooking, cut white fish into serving pieces. Using a stiff

brush, thoroughly scrub the mussels, cutting off their beards, or soak clams in cold water to which a little cornmeal has been added and then scrub under cold running water to remove any residue of mud and sand. Stir wine into tomato mixture. Add white fish, shrimp, and scallops.

6. Cook, covered, on HIGH for 10 minutes.
7. Place mussels or clams in a layer on top of fish in casserole.
8. Cook, covered, on HIGH for 10 minutes, or until shells are fully opened.
9. Discard any mussels or clams that are unopened.
10. Ladle soup into soup plates. Sprinkle with parsley and serve piping hot with French bread.

Clam Chowder   3 to 4 servings

2 slices bacon
1 can (7 ounces) minced clams, with liquid
1 large potato, peeled and cubed

¼ cup minced onion
1 can (13 ounces) evaporated milk
Salt and pepper to taste
1 tablespoon butter

1. Put bacon slices in a 2-quart casserole. Cover with a piece of paper towel.
2. Cook on HIGH for 3 minutes, or until bacon is crisp.
3. Remove paper towel and bacon, leaving drippings in casserole. Crumble bacon into bits and reserve. Add clams, clam liquid, potato, onion, and ½ cup water to casserole.
4. Cook, covered, on HIGH for 9 minutes, or until potatoes are tender.
5. Add milk, crumbled bacon, salt and pepper to taste, and butter.
6. Cook, covered, on HIGH for 3 minutes, or just until mixture comes to a boil.
7. Let stand 2 minutes. Serve with crumbled common crackers if desired.

Red Bean Soup   6 servings

8 slices bacon
2 tablespoons bacon drippings
1 large onion, diced
1 clove garlic, crushed

2 cans (27 ounces each) red kidney beans
½ teaspoon salt
1 can (8 ounces) tomato sauce

1. Cook bacon according to directions on page 60. Crumble and reserve.
2. Place bacon drippings in a 2-quart casserole. Add onion and garlic and cook, covered, on HIGH for 2 minutes.
3. Add ½ cup water and remaining ingredients, including liquid from the canned beans. Mix well.
4. Cook, covered, on HIGH for 5 to 6 minutes to blend flavors.
5. Puree soup in a blender, half at a time, and return to casserole. If soup is too thick, stir in enough water to make it the desired consistency.
6. Cook on BAKE for 3 minutes, or until piping hot.
7. Stir in reserved bacon before serving.

Quebec Green Pea Soup
4 to 6 servings

1 can (2 ounces) mushroom stems
and pieces
1 tablespoon butter or margarine

2 cans (11½ ounces) condensed
green pea soup, undiluted
1 cup grated raw carrots

1. Drain mushrooms, pouring liquid into a measuring cup. Add enough water to make 2 cups of liquid.
2. Melt butter in a 1½- to 2-quart casserole on BAKE for 30 seconds. Add drained mushrooms.
3. Cook on HIGH for 3 minutes, or just until heated.
4. Add soup and mushroom-water mixture. Stir until well blended. Stir in grated carrots.
5. Cook, covered, on ROAST for 7 to 9 minutes, or just until carrots are crisply tender.
6. Taste and season if necessary. Serve with croutons or crackers.

Spring Pea Soup
4 servings

1 package (10 ounces) frozen peas
3 cups chicken broth
6 scallions, sliced

¼ teaspoon white pepper
½ cup heavy cream

1. Place peas in a 1½-quart ovenproof casserole. Add chicken broth, scallions, and pepper.
2. Cook, covered, on HIGH for 7 minutes, stirring once.
3. Stir in cream, taste, and add salt if necessary.
4. Cook on BAKE for 1 minute.

Note: If desired, after Step 2, puree soup in a blender or force through a sieve. Proceed with Step 3.

Chili Chowder
6 servings

¾ pound ground beef
1 medium onion, chopped
1 clove garlic, chopped
2 tablespoons chopped green pepper
1 can (1 pound) peeled plum tomatoes

2 cups tomato juice
1 teaspoon salt
⅛ teaspoon sugar
2 teaspoons chili powder, or to taste

1. Place beef, onion, garlic, and green pepper in a 2-quart ovenproof casserole.
2. Cook, covered, on HIGH for 4 minutes.
3. Remove casserole and stir contents to break up beef.
4. Add tomatoes, including liquid from can, stirring to break up tomatoes.
5. Add remaining ingredients and mix well.
6. Cook, covered, on HIGH for 7 minutes, or until piping hot.

Meats

Roasts, chops, hamburgers, and small cuts of tender meat cook beautifully in the microwave oven. Pot roasts and tough cuts that require long, slow cooking will do better in the conventional range or oven.

A large piece of meat, especially if the shape is uneven, should be turned and rotated for uniform roasting. If overdone spots appear, cover with small pieces of aluminum foil to slow or halt the cooking in these places. Be sure to remove the roast before it reaches "done" temperature, as it continues to cook after being removed from the microwave oven. Let it stand until the desired degree of doneness is reached. If the meat does not reach the temperature desired, it is a simple matter to return it to the microwave oven for just a few minutes longer.

HOW TO THAW MEAT, POULTRY, OR FISH

Place meat or poultry or fish that is to be thawed in a glass dish. Set microwave oven to DEFROST unless otherwise specified, and then follow the table below for cooking and standing times.

Beef

Ground (frozen in a flat square)	5½–6½ minutes per pound (turn once)	stand 5 minutes
Round steak	3½–5½ minutes per pound (turn once)	stand 10 minutes
Rump roast	5–6 minutes per pound (turn once)	stand 30 minutes
Sirloin steak, ½ inch thick	6–8 minutes per pound (turn once)	stand 20–30 minutes
Standing rib roast	6–7 minutes per pound (turn once)	stand 1 hour
Lamb or Pork Chops	3–4 minutes per pound, separate chops, then 1 more minute per pound	stand 10–15 minutes
Chicken		
cut in pieces	5 minutes per pound (turn every 5 minutes), separate pieces, then 3–5 more minutes per pound	stand 10 minutes
Fish		
Filets	4 minutes per pound, separate filets, then 2 more minutes per pound	stand 5 minutes

FOR ROASTING MEATS REFER TO CHART ON PAGE xv, FOR POULTRY, PAGE xvi.

Frozen Pot Roast   4 to 6 servings

2½ to 3 pounds bottom round roast, frozen
3 carrots, cleaned and cut in chunks
2 onions, cut in eighths
2 large potatoes, cut in chunks
1 envelope (⅞ ounce) onion gravy mix

1. Place frozen round roast in a 2- to 3-quart casserole. Cover tightly and cook on SIMMER for 20 minutes.
2. Turn meat over. Cover tightly and cook on SIMMER for 20 minutes.

3. Turn meat over. Add vegetables. Sprinkle gravy mix over top of meat and vegetables. Cook on SIMMER for 15 minutes.
4. Turn meat over. Stir vegetables lightly. Cook on SIMMER for 15 minutes more, or until meat and vegetables are tender.

Oriental Beef   4 to 6 servings

1½ to 2 pounds thinly cut boneless sirloin steak, cut into thin strips
½ cup soy sauce
¼ cup dry sherry
¼ cup water
1 tablespoon sugar

1 whole clove garlic
2 thin slices ginger
1 bunch green onions
1 can (5 ounces) water chestnuts
½ bunch fresh broccoli
½ pound fresh bean sprouts

1. Combine steak, soy sauce, sherry, water, sugar, garlic, and ginger in a 12- by 7-inch glass baking dish. Cover with plastic wrap and let stand at room temperature 4 hours. Occasionally, uncover and turn meat over.
2. Clean green onions and cut into 2-inch pieces. Drain water chestnuts and slice. Peel broccoli and cut stems into very thin slices. Leave flowerets whole. Rinse bean sprouts.
3. Remove garlic and ginger from meat. Place some of each vegetable in each corner of the baking dish. Cover dish with plastic wrap.
4. Cook on HIGH for 10 to 12 minutes. Remove and let stand 2 minutes.
5. Serve with hot cooked rice.

Beef Stroganoff   6 to 8 servings

¼ cup butter or margarine
3 large onions, thinly sliced
1 tablespoon mustard
1 teaspoon salt
Grind of fresh pepper
2 pounds top round steak, cut into thin strips

2 cans (4 ounces each) mushroom stems and pieces, drained
1 cup dairy sour cream
Hot buttered noodles or rice

1. Combine butter, onions, mustard, salt, and pepper in a 3-quart glass casserole. Cover and cook on SAUTE for 5 minutes, or until onion is limp.
2. Add beef. Cover and cook on HIGH for 10 minutes; stir once during cooking time.
3. Add mushrooms. Cover and cook on SIMMER for 20 to 25 minutes, or until meat is tender. Stir once or twice during cooking time.
4. Add sour cream. Cover and cook on DEFROST for 5 minutes, or just until sauce is heated. Let stand 5 minutes.
5. Serve with noodles or rice.

FOLLOWING PAGES: Left, *Standing Ribs of Beef*; right, *Beef Tacos, page 47.*

Beef Goulash

4 servings

2 pounds stew beef, cut in 1-inch cubes

3 to 4 large tomatoes

1 onion, coarsely chopped

1 teaspoon salt

½ teaspoon freshly ground pepper

1 cup sour cream (optional)

1. Place beef in a 2- to 3-quart casserole.
2. Peel tomatoes; remove cores. Cut tomatoes in chunks. Place in casserole with beef, onion, salt, and pepper. Toss mixture lightly.
3. Cook, covered, on REHEAT for 40 to 45 minutes, or until beef is tender. Stir occasionally during cooking period.
4. If desired, stir sour cream into mixture and let stand, covered, 5 minutes.

Note: This is excellent served with cooked egg noodles.

Beef Casserole

4 servings

1 package (10 ounces) frozen French-style green beans

1 pound stew beef, cut in cubes

½ teaspoon meat tenderizer

1 large onion, chopped

1 can (10½ ounces) condensed tomato soup, undiluted

2 cups cooked egg noodles

Salt and pepper

1. Place green beans in a 1-quart casserole, icy side up.
2. Cook, covered, on HIGH for 5 minutes. Reserve.
3. Combine beef cubes and meat tenderizer in a 2- to 3-quart casserole. Toss lightly. Add onion.
4. Cook, covered, on HIGH for 15 to 20 minutes, or until meat is tender.
5. Add tomato soup, ½ cup water, noodles, and green beans to beef cubes. Stir lightly and season with salt and pepper to taste.
6. Cook, covered, on HIGH for 5 minutes.
7. Stir and let stand, covered, 3 to 4 minutes before serving.

Short Ribs of Beef

4 servings

2 pounds meaty short ribs of beef

1 clove garlic, minced

½ teaspoon salt

½ cup dry red wine

1 tablespoon liquid gravy seasoning

1. Arrange short ribs in a 2- or 3-quart casserole. Sprinkle with garlic and salt. Combine wine and liquid gravy seasoning. Pour over short ribs.
2. Cook, covered, on ROAST for about 30 minutes, or until meat is tender, stirring once or twice during cooking period.
3. Remove and let stand 5 minutes.

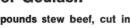

Tomato Swiss Steak

4 servings

¼ cup all-purpose flour
1 teaspoon salt
¼ teaspoon pepper
1½ to 2 pounds round steak

2 large onions, sliced
1 can (10½ ounces) condensed
   tomato soup, undiluted
1 can (8 ounces) tomato sauce

1. Combine flour, salt, and pepper. Place steak on a board and pound half of the flour mixture into each side of steak with the back of a heavy knife. Cut meat in 4 pieces and place in an 8-inch baking dish. Sprinkle any remaining flour over top of meat. Spread onion over meat. Combine tomato soup and tomato sauce with ½ cup water. Pour over steak.
2. Cook, covered, on HIGH for 5 minutes. Cook on BAKE for 20 minutes. Turn meat over. Cook, covered, on BAKE for 20 minutes, or until meat is tender.

Onion Steak

4 servings

¼ cup all-purpose flour
1 teaspoon salt
¼ teaspoon pepper

1½ to 2 pounds round steak
½ package (1⅓ ounces) onion soup mix

1. Combine flour, salt, and pepper. Place steak on a board and pound half of the flour mixture into each side of steak with the back of a heavy knife. Cut meat in 4 pieces and place in an 8-inch baking dish. Sprinkle any remaining flour over top of meat. Combine onion soup mix with 1 cup water. Pour over top of meat.
2. Cook, covered, on HIGH for 5 minutes. Cook on BAKE for 20 minutes. Turn meat over. Cook, covered, on BAKE for 20 minutes, or until meat is tender.

Beef Stew

4 to 6 servings

2 pounds stew meat, cut in 1-inch
   cubes
½ teaspoon meat tenderizer
½ teaspoon salt
1 package (1½ ounces) brown gravy
   mix with mushrooms

3 stalks celery, cut in pieces
3 medium carrots, cut in small chunks
2 medium potatoes, peeled and cut in
   eighths

1. Put beef cubes in a 3-quart casserole. Sprinkle with meat tenderizer and salt. Combine gravy mix with 1 cup water and stir well. Pour over meat.
2. Cook, covered, on HIGH for 5 minutes. Cook, covered, on BAKE for 20 minutes.
3. Add celery, carrots, and potatoes and stir lightly so that vegetables are covered with gravy. Add more water for a thinner gravy and a little additional salt for the vegetables, if desired.
4. Cook, covered, on BAKE for about 20 minutes, or until vegetables and meat are tender.
5. Remove and let stand 5 minutes.

FOLLOWING PAGES: Left, *Beef Stew, page 35;* right, *Shish Kabob, page 38.*

Shish Kabob

6 to 8 servings

½ cup wine vinegar
½ cup cooking oil
1 teaspoon onion salt
1 clove garlic, split in half
¼ cup soy sauce
2 teaspoons Italian seasoning
2 pounds boneless sirloin or top round steak

½ pound small fresh mushrooms
1 dozen tomato wedges or cherry tomatoes
1 green pepper, seeded and cut in 1-inch squares

1. Combine vinegar, oil, onion salt, garlic, soy sauce, Italian seasoning, and ½ cup water in a large mixing bowl. Cut steak in 1-inch cubes. Add to marinade and let stand at room temperature 5 to 6 hours.
2. Place meat cubes and desired vegetables alternately on long wooden skewers.
3. Place 2 or 3 skewers on a dinner plate.
4. Cook, uncovered, on HIGH for 3 minutes for medium rare. Cook slightly longer for well-done meat.

Note: The marinade turns the meat brown while standing, for attractive color in the finished kabobs.

Beef and Peppers

4 servings

2 tablespoons cooking oil
1 pound top round or sirloin steak, cut into thin strips
1 medium onion, finely chopped
1 clove garlic, minced
1 teaspoon salt

⅛ teaspoon pepper
1 can (1 pound) tomatoes, broken up
2 large green peppers, seeded and cut in strips
2 tablespoons soy sauce

1. Put oil in a 2- or 3-quart casserole or baking dish. Add beef strips and toss lightly so that meat is coated with oil. Add onion, garlic, salt, and pepper.
2. Cook, covered, on HIGH for about 5 minutes, stirring once during cooking time.
3. Add tomatoes. Cook, covered, on HIGH for 4 minutes, stirring once during cooking time.
4. Add green pepper strips and soy sauce and toss thoroughly.
5. Cook, covered, on HIGH for 4 to 5 minutes, or just until green pepper is tender.
6. Serve with hot cooked rice or chow mein noodles.

Nutty Meatballs

4 servings

1 pound lean ground beef
1 egg, lightly beaten
¼ cup milk
½ cup soft bread crumbs
½ cup chopped pecans

2 tablespoons chopped parsley
½ teaspoon salt
Freshly ground pepper to taste
1 can (10½ ounces) condensed tomato
   soup, undiluted

1. Combine ground beef with egg, milk, bread crumbs, pecans, parsley, salt, and pepper. Blend well. Shape mixture into 24 meatballs. Arrange in an oblong baking dish.
2. Cook, covered, on ROAST for 5 minutes.
3. Turn meatballs over. Cook, covered, on ROAST for 2 minutes.
4. Drain off fat and liquid. Add tomato soup. Blend lightly. Cook, covered, on ROAST for 3 minutes, or until piping hot, stirring once during cooking time.
5. Let stand 5 minutes before serving.
6. Serve over hot mashed potatoes.

Beef Rolls

6 servings

2 pounds beef top round steak, cut ½
   inch thick
2 tablespoons butter or margarine
½ cup chopped celery with leaves
¼ cup chopped onion
1 cup soft bread crumbs

¼ teaspoon crushed rosemary
¼ teaspoon thyme
Grind of fresh pepper
1 can (10½ ounces) condensed
   cream of mushroom soup

1. Pound steak lightly with the side of a cleaver or a meat pounder. Cut into 6 pieces.
2. Combine butter, celery, and onion in a 1-quart glass measure. Cook on HIGH for 4 minutes, or until onion is limp. Remove from oven. Stir in bread crumbs, rosemary, thyme, and pepper.
3. Divide stuffing among pieces of steak. Roll meat around stuffing and fasten with toothpicks. Arrange in a glass baking dish. Spoon soup over top of meat rolls.
4. Cook on ROAST for 20 minutes, or until meat is tender. Rearrange meat once during cooking time, spooning sauce over top of meat rolls.
5. Let stand 5 minutes before serving.

Onion Meatballs

6 servings

1½ pounds lean ground beef
½ cup milk
1 package (1¼ ounces) onion soup mix

3 tablespoons all-purpose flour
2 tablespoons chopped parsley
½ cup dairy sour cream

1. In a large bowl combine beef with milk and 2 tablespoons of the onion soup mix. Mix thoroughly. Shape into 24 meatballs. Place in a 3-quart oblong baking dish.
2. Cook, covered, on HIGH for 3 minutes.
3. Turn meatballs over. Cook, covered, on HIGH for 2 minutes.
4. Remove meatballs. Stir flour into drippings in dish. Stir in 1½ cups water, parsley, and remaining soup mix.
5. Cook, uncovered, on BAKE for about 5 minutes, or until mixture comes to a boil.
6. Add meatballs. Cook, covered, on BAKE for 6 minutes, stirring occasionally during cooking time.
7. Gradually blend in sour cream. Cover and let stand 5 minutes before serving.
8. Serve over rice or noodles.

Meatballs Stroganoff

5 to 6 servings

¾ cup milk
3 slices bread, cubed
1 pound ground beef
1 egg, lightly beaten
3 tablespoons grated onion
3 tablespoons dried parsley flakes
1 teaspoon salt

Freshly ground pepper to taste
3 tablespoons flour
1½ cups beef broth or bouillon
1 tablespoon tomato paste
¼ teaspoon paprika
1½ cups dairy sour cream

1. Pour milk into a mixing bowl. Cook in oven on ROAST for about 1 minute, or just long enough to warm milk.
2. Add bread cubes and mix until all the milk is absorbed by the bread.
3. Add beef, egg, onion, parsley, salt, and pepper. Blend well. Form mixture into balls about 1½ inches in diameter. Arrange meatballs in a 7¼- by 11¾-inch oblong baking dish.
4. Cook, covered, on HIGH for 3 minutes.
5. Turn meatballs over. Cook, covered, on HIGH for 2 minutes. Drain off fat and liquid.
6. Stir together flour and beef broth to make a smooth mixture. Stir in tomato paste and paprika. Pour mixture over top of meatballs.
7. Cook, covered, on BAKE for 5 minutes, stirring occasionally.
8. Top with sour cream and stir lightly. Cover and cook on LOW for 5 minutes, or until serving time.
9. Serve with cooked rice or hot buttered noddles.

OPPOSITE: *Beef and Peppers, page 38.*

Herbed Meat Loaf
6 servings

2 eggs, lightly beaten
¼ cup bread crumbs
1 tablespoon chopped parsley
¼ cup chopped chives or onion
1 tablespoon dried basil
¼ cup chopped green pepper

1½ teaspoons salt
½ teaspoon pepper
1 pound ground beef
½ pound ground veal
½ pound lean ground pork

1. Combine all ingredients except meat, and mix well. Add ground meat and blend with hands, being careful not to mix more than necessary.
2. Shape into a round and place in an 8-inch pie plate. Make a depression in center of loaf.
3. Cook, uncovered, on ROAST for 25 minutes, or until center of loaf is cooked.
4. Remove. Cover meat and let stand 10 minutes before serving.
5. Serve with mushroom gravy or tomato sauce, if desired.

Note: Use caution when slicing, since meat juices tend to squirt when meat is sliced.

Our Favorite Meat Loaf
6 servings

1 can (8 ounces) tomato sauce
¼ cup brown sugar
¼ cup vinegar
1 teaspoon prepared mustard
1 egg, lightly beaten

1 medium onion, minced
¼ cup cracker crumbs
2 pounds ground beef
1½ teaspoons salt
¼ teaspoon pepper

1. Combine tomato sauce, brown sugar, vinegar, and mustard in a small bowl. Set aside.
2. Combine egg, onion, cracker crumbs, ground beef, salt, and pepper in a mixing bowl. Add ½ cup of the tomato mixture and blend thoroughly. Shape into an oval loaf and place in an oblong baking dish. Make a depression in top of loaf. Pour remaining tomato sauce over top of meat.
3. Cook, uncovered, on ROAST for 25 to 30 minutes, or until center is cooked.
4. Cover meat and let stand about 10 minutes before serving.

Vegetable Meat Loaf
6 servings

1 can (10½ ounces) condensed vegetable soup, undiluted
2 pounds lean ground beef
½ cup fine dry bread crumbs
½ cup chopped onions
2 tablespoons chopped parsley

1 tablespoon Worcestershire sauce
1 egg, lightly beaten
1 teaspoon salt
Freshly ground pepper to taste
4 tomato slices
½ cup grated process American cheese

1. Combine soup, beef, bread crumbs, onion, parsley, Worcestershire, egg, salt, and pepper. Mix thoroughly. Shape into an oval loaf and place in an oblong baking dish. Make a slight depression in the top of the loaf.

2. Cook, covered with a piece of waxed paper, on ROAST for 25 to 30 minutes, or until center of loaf is done.
3. Place tomato slices and cheese on top of loaf. Cook, uncovered, on BRAISE for 5 minutes, or until cheese is melted.
4. Let stand at WARM for 5 minutes before serving.

Vintage Meat Loaf   6 servings

2 tablespoons dry red wine	2 tablespoons minced onion
2 tablespoons milk	¾ teaspoon salt
1 cup soft bread crumbs	Freshly ground pepper to taste
2 pounds lean ground beef	½ teaspoon dry mustard
1 egg, lightly beaten	½ teaspoon mixed herbs

1. Put red wine and milk in a mixing bowl with bread crumbs. Let stand a few minutes for bread to absorb the liquid. Add beef, egg, onion, salt, pepper, mustard, and herbs. Mix lightly until completely blended. Pack mixture in an 8- by 4- by 3-inch loaf dish.
2. Cover loaf with a piece of waxed paper. Cook, covered, on ROAST for 17 minutes, or until meat is done in center.
3. Remove and let stand, covered, 5 minutes before serving.

Cabbage Rolls   6 to 8 servings

1 head cabbage, about 1½ pounds	1 tablespoon chopped parsley
1 pound ground beef	1 clove garlic, minced
½ pound ground pork	2 teaspoons salt
¾ cup cooked rice	¼ teaspoon pepper
1 egg, lightly beaten	¼ cup butter or margarine
1 teaspoon thyme	1 can (16 ounces) tomato sauce

1. Remove core from cabbage. Remove any blemished leaves. Put cabbage in a 3-quart casserole. Add boiling water to cover about one-quarter of the bottom of the cabbage.
2. Cook, covered, on HIGH for 6 minutes.
3. Cool cabbage slightly and remove 6 to 8 of the large outside leaves. Remove the tough center core from each leaf.
4. Combine ground beef, pork, rice, egg, thyme, parsley, garlic, salt, and pepper. Toss together lightly. Divide mixture among cabbage leaves. Wrap leaves tightly around mixture.
5. Line bottom of a 3-quart casserole with some of the leftover cabbage leaves. Place rolled cabbage packets on top of loose leaves. Cover with remaining pieces of cabbage.
6. Top with butter. Pour tomato sauce over top.
7. Cook, covered, on REHEAT for about 30 minutes, or until meat is cooked and rolls are fork-tender.
8. Remove and let stand, covered, 10 minutes.
9. Discard the top loose cabbage leaves before serving.

FOLLOWING PAGES: Left, *Chili con Carne*, page 46; right, *Curried Lamb*, page 51.

Broccoli and Beef

2 servings

1 large or 2 medium stalks broccoli
2 tablespoons cooking oil
½ cup coarsely chopped onions
1 clove garlic, minced

½ pound ground beef
½ cup thinly sliced celery
2 teaspoons soy sauce
1 tablespoon dry sherry

1. Cut off flowerets from top of broccoli and cut large flowers in halves or quarters. Peel broccoli stalks and cut in diagonal slices about ½ inch thick. Set aside.
2. In a 1½-quart casserole place oil, onion, and garlic. Add beef, broken into pieces.
3. Cook, covered, on HIGH for 4 minutes.
4. Remove casserole and break up pieces of beef with a fork. Add celery, soy sauce, sherry, and broccoli. Stir.
5. Cook, covered, on REHEAT for 8 to 9 minutes, or just until broccoli is crisply tender.
6. Serve over hot cooked rice with additional soy sauce.

Hamburger Hash Burgundy

4 servings

1 pound ground beef
½ cup chopped onions
2 tablespoons all-purpose flour
1 can (10½ ounces) condensed beef consomme, undiluted

½ cup dry red wine
2 cups diced raw potatoes
½ cup diced celery
Salt and pepper to taste

1. Crumble ground beef into a 2-quart casserole. Stir in onion.
2. Cook, uncovered, on HIGH for 2 minutes.
3. Stir with a fork to break up meat. Cook on HIGH for 4 minutes, or until meat loses its red color.
4. Sprinkle flour on meat. Stir in well. Add consomme and wine.
5. Cook, covered, on HIGH for 5 minutes.
6. Add potatoes and celery, and salt and pepper to taste.
7. Cook, covered, on BAKE for 15 to 20 minutes, or until potatoes are tender.
8. Let stand 5 minutes before serving.

Chili con Carne

4 servings

1 pound ground beef
½ cup chopped onions
1 clove garlic, minced
2 to 3 teaspoons chili powder

1 teaspoon salt
1 can (16 ounces) tomato sauce
1 can (1 pound) kidney beans

1. Crumble ground beef in a 2-quart casserole. Add onion and garlic.
2. Cook, uncovered, on HIGH for 4 minutes. Break up meat with a fork.
3. Add remaining ingredients. Cook, covered, on BAKE for 10 to 12 minutes, or until piping hot. Stir once during cooking period.

Variation: Omit chili powder and salt and use half a package (1¾ ounces) chili mix.

46

Limas and Beef Casserole

4 to 6 servings

- 1 pound lean ground beef
- 1 clove garlic, crushed
- 1 medium onion, chopped
- 1 small green pepper, seeded and chopped
- ¼ teaspoon chili powder
- ½ teaspoon dry mustard
- 2 teaspoons Worcestershire sauce
- ½ teaspoon salt
- 2 cans (1 pound each) lima beans
- 1 can (8 ounces) tomato sauce

1. Combine beef, garlic, onion, and green pepper in a 2- or 3-quart casserole.
2. Cook, uncovered, on HIGH for 5 minutes. Stir with a fork to break up meat.
3. Add remaining ingredients. Toss lightly.
4. Cook, covered, on HIGH for 6 minutes, stirring once during cooking period.
5. Let stand, covered, 3 to 4 minutes before serving.

Beef Tacos

10 to 12 servings

- 1 pound ground beef
- ½ cup chopped onions
- 1 can (8 ounces) tomato sauce
- ¼ teaspoon chili powder
- ¼ teaspoon salt
- ¼ teaspoon garlic salt
- 10 to 12 fully cooked taco shells
- Grated Cheddar cheese
- Shredded lettuce
- Chopped fresh tomato
- Finely diced avocado

1. Crumble beef into a 1-quart casserole. Add onion.
2. Cook, uncovered, on HIGH for 4 minutes. Stir with a fork to break up meat.
3. Add tomato sauce, chili powder, salt, and garlic salt.
4. Cover casserole with a paper towel. Cook for about 5 minutes, or until sauce is blended and thickened.
5. Cook, covered, on BAKE for 6 to 7 minutes.
6. Spoon filling into taco shells. Serve immediately with cheese, lettuce, tomato, and avocado in side dishes to sprinkle over top of hot filling.

FOLLOWING PAGES: Left, *Veal Parmigiana, page 54;* right, *Barbecued Spareribs, page 58.*

Burger Stroganoff

4 to 6 servings

1 pound ground beef
½ cup minced onions
1 clove garlic, minced
1 pound fresh mushrooms, sliced

2 teaspoons salt
¼ teaspoon pepper
2 tablespoons all-purpose flour
1 cup dairy sour cream

1. Crumble beef into a 1½-quart casserole. Add onion and garlic.
2. Cook, uncovered, on HIGH for 2 minutes. Stir lightly.
3. Cook, uncovered, on HIGH for 2 minutes.
4. Add mushrooms. Cook, covered, on HIGH for 2 minutes.
5. Sprinkle salt, pepper, and flour over top of meat. Stir well.
6. Cook, covered, on HIGH for 3 minutes, stirring once during cooking period.
7. Stir in sour cream. Cook, covered, on WARM for 3 minutes, or just long enough to warm the sour cream mixture. It can be left in oven on WARM for several minutes before serving.
8. Serve over hot cooked noodles or mashed potatoes.

Leg of Lamb

8 servings

4- to 4½-pound leg of lamb, bone in   1 large clove garlic, cut in thin slices

1. Cut small slits in both sides of leg of lamb. Insert thin slices of garlic in slits.
2. Place leg of lamb, fat side down, on a microwave roasting rack in an oblong baking dish. Use an inverted saucer if there is no rack.
3. Cook, uncovered, on HIGH for 25 minutes.
4. Turn lamb over with fat side up. Insert a microwave meat thermometer in thickest part of leg, making sure not to touch the bone. Cook, uncovered, on ROAST for about 20 minutes, or until thermometer registers 160° F. Remove from oven, insert a standard meat thermometer into meat to register 160° F.
5. Cover with aluminum foil and let stand, about 20 minutes, until thermometer reaches desired temperature and to make the meat easier to carve.

Note: Cooking time for leg of lamb averages 9 to 11 minutes per pound.

Zesty Lamb Chops

4 servings

4 shoulder lamb chops
½ cup coarsely chopped onion
1 clove garlic, minced

½ cup catsup
2 tablespoons Worcestershire sauce
1 tablespoon prepared mustard

1. In a baking dish arrange lamb chops in one layer. Sprinkle with onion and garlic. Cook, uncovered, on HIGH for 5 minutes.
2. Combine remaining ingredients and spread over lamb chops. Cook, covered, on BAKE for 15 minutes, or until lamb chops are tender.

Lamb Stew

4 servings

1 pound boneless lamb, cut in 1-inch cubes
1 package (⅝ ounce) brown gravy mix
2 tablespoons all-purpose flour
1 teaspoon salt
⅛ teaspoon pepper

1 clove garlic, minced
½ teaspoon Worcestershire sauce
¼ cup red wine
3 medium carrots, peeled and cut in chunks
2 stalks celery, cut in pieces
2 potatoes, peeled and cut in cubes

1. In a 2- or 3-quart casserole combine lamb and gravy mix.
2. Cook, uncovered, on HIGH for 5 minutes, stirring occasionally.
3. Add remaining ingredients, with 1 cup of water. Stir well.
4. Cook, covered, on BAKE for 20 to 25 minutes, or until meat and vegetables are tender. Stir once during cooking period.
5. Let stand 3 to 4 minutes before serving.

Curried Lamb

4 servings

1 pound boneless lamb, cut in 1-inch cubes
2 tablespoons all-purpose flour
1 clove garlic, minced
1 large onion, sliced
¼ cup butter or margarine

1½ tablespoons curry powder
2 apples, peeled, cored, and chopped in coarse pieces
2 tablespoons seedless raisins
1½ teaspoons salt

1. Toss lamb cubes lightly with flour. Set aside.
2. Place garlic, onion, butter, and curry powder in a 2-quart casserole. Cook, uncovered, on HIGH for 3 to 4 minutes.
3. Add lamb and toss lightly.
4. Cook, uncovered, on HIGH for 3 minutes, stirring once.
5. Add apples, raisins, and salt. Stir in ½ cup water.
6. Cook, covered, on BAKE for 20 to 25 minutes, or until meat is tender. Stir once during cooking period.
7. Cook, covered, on WARM for 5 minutes.
8. Serve with hot cooked rice and accompaniments such as flaked coconut, chopped peanuts or walnuts, and chutney.

FOLLOWING PAGES: Left, *Sweet and Sour Pork, page 58;* right, *Stuffed Pork Chops, page 57.*

Veal Elegante

3 to 4 servings

1 pound boneless veal, cut in cubes
½ cup minced onions
1 fresh tomato, peeled and cubed

½ cup dry white wine
Salt and pepper to taste

1. Combine veal, onion, tomatoes, wine, and salt and pepper to taste in a 1½-quart casserole.
2. Cook, covered, on HIGH for 15 minutes, or until veal is tender. Stir once during cooking period.
3. Let stand 3 to 4 minutes. Serve over hot cooked rice or cooked buttered noodles.

Veal Parmigiana

4 servings

1 egg, lightly beaten
¼ teaspoon salt
3 tablespoons cracker crumbs
⅓ cup grated Parmesan cheese
1 pound veal cutlets
2 tablespoons cooking oil
¼ cup dry vermouth

1 medium onion, chopped
1 cup (4 ounces) sliced or shredded
  mozzarella cheese
1 can (8 ounces) tomato sauce
Grind of fresh pepper
⅛ teaspoon oregano

1. Beat egg with salt in a shallow dish. Combine cracker crumbs and Parmesan cheese on a piece of waxed paper. Cut veal into 4 serving pieces. Place each piece between two pieces of waxed paper and pound to about ¼ inch thick with the side of a cleaver.
2. Dip veal in egg and then in cracker crumbs. Heat oil in a skillet on top of the range. Cook veal in hot oil until golden brown on both sides.
3. Place veal in a 10- by 6-inch baking dish. Add vermouth to skillet and heat about 1 minute, scraping up browned bits from bottom of skillet. Pour over veal cutlets.
4. Sprinkle onion over meat. Top with mozzarella cheese. Spoon tomato sauce over top, and season with pepper and oregano.
5. Cook, covered, on BAKE for 10 minutes, or until sauce is bubbly and cheese is melted.

Cordon Bleu Veal

2 servings

½ pound veal round steak or cutlets,
  cut ½-inch thick
1 slice Swiss cheese
2 thin slices boiled ham
1½ tablespoons all-purpose flour

1 egg
¼ cup dry bread crumbs
1½ tablespoons butter or margarine
1 tablespoon chopped parsley
1 tablespoon dry white wine

1. Cut veal into 4 pieces. Place each piece of veal between 2 sheets of waxed paper and pound with the side of a cleaver or a mallet until veal is ⅛ inch thick.
2. Cut cheese in 2 pieces. Fold each piece of cheese in half. Place on a slice of

ham. Roll ham around cheese three times so that finished roll of ham is smaller than the pieces of veal. Place ham on one slice of veal and top with a second slice. Press edges of veal together to seal.

3. Put flour on a piece of waxed paper. Beat egg lightly with 1 tablespoon water. Put bread crumbs on a piece of waxed paper. Dip veal in flour, then in beaten egg, and finally coat well with bread crumbs.
4. Put butter and parsley in an 8-inch baking dish.
5. Cook in oven for 1 minute, or just long enough to heat butter well.
6. Add veal to very hot butter.
7. Cook, uncovered, on HIGH for 2 minutes. Turn veal slices over.
8. Cook, uncovered, on HIGH for 2 minutes, or just until veal is tender.
9. Pour wine over veal and tilt pan to swish wine around. Serve immediately.

Loin of Pork   6 to 8 servings

1 loin of pork, about 4 pounds, bone in

1. Cook, uncovered, on HIGH for 5 minutes.
2. Cook, uncovered, on BAKE for 15 minutes.
3. Turn roast fat side up. Cook on BAKE for 20 to 25 minutes, or until the internal temperature of thickest part of meat registers 165° F on a meat thermometer.
4. Let stand, covered with foil, until meat thermometer registers 185° F.

Note: Do not use a meat thermometer in a microwave oven. You may use the special thermometer designed for microwave ovens.
Generally, the cooking time for roast pork is from 10 to 12 minutes per pound, with the oven set on BAKE.

Orange Ginger Pork Chops   6 servings

6 lean pork chops	1 teaspoon ground ginger
¼ cup orange juice	1 large orange, peeled and sliced
½ teaspoon salt	Dairy sour cream

1. Trim fat from pork chops. Place in an oblong baking dish. Pour orange juice over chops.
2. Cook, covered, on HIGH for 10 minutes.
3. Remove from oven. Turn chops over. Sprinkle with salt and ginger. Place an orange slice on top of each chop.
4. Cook, covered, on HIGH for 10 minutes.
5. Remove from oven. Top each chop with a dollop of sour cream. Cover and let stand 5 minutes before serving.

Pork Chops with Apricots

4 servings

4 center-cut pork chops, about 1½ pounds
2 tablespoons brown sugar

½ teaspoon oregano
Salt and pepper to taste
1 can (8¾ ounces) apricot halves

1. Trim all fat from pork chops. Place chops in an 8-inch square baking dish. Sprinkle brown sugar, oregano, salt, and pepper on each chop. Pour half of the liquid from the apricots over chops.
2. Cook, covered, on HIGH for 10 minutes.
3. Spoon some of liquid over top of chops. Top with apricots.
4. Cook, covered, on HIGH for 10 minutes, or until pork is tender.
5. Let stand 5 minutes before serving.

Stuffed Pork Chops

4 servings

1 cup coarse dry bread crumbs
¾ cup chopped apples
3 tablespoons chopped raisins
½ teaspoon salt
2 tablespoons sugar
2 tablespoons finely minced onion

Freshly ground pepper to taste
Pinch of sage
2 tablespoons melted butter or margarine
8 thin rib or loin pork chops
½ package (⅝ ounce) brown gravy mix

1. Combine bread crumbs, apples, raisins, salt, sugar, onion, pepper, sage, and melted butter. Toss together lightly. Moisten slightly with hot water if stuffing is dry.
2. Trim all fat from pork chops. Place 4 chops in bottom of an 8-inch square baking dish. Divide stuffing into 4 portions and place one portion on top of each chop. Cover chops with 4 remaining chops, pressing together lightly.
3. Sprinkle brown gravy mix over top of chops. (To make an even layer, sift mixture through a small strainer.)
4. Cook, uncovered, on HIGH for 15 minutes, or just until pork is tender. Do not overcook.

Tomatoed Pork Chops

4 servings

4 center-cut pork chops
1 large onion, sliced
1 can (15 ounces) tomato sauce

Dash of hot-pepper sauce
¼ teaspoon marjoram

1. Trim all fat from chops. Place chops in an 8-inch square baking dish. Cover with sliced onion. Combine tomato sauce, hot-pepper sauce, and marjoram. Pour mixture over chops.
2. Cook, covered, on HIGH for 10 minutes.
3. Remove from oven. Turn chops over. Spoon some of the sauce in bottom of dish over chops.
4. Cook, covered, on HIGH for 10 minutes.
5. Allow to stand 5 minutes before serving.

OPPOSITE: *Baked Ham Steak, page 59.*

Sweet and Sour Pork
6 servings

1½ pounds lean pork shoulder, cut in
   ½-inch cubes
 1 small onion, sliced
 1 teaspoon salt
 1 can (8 ounces) pineapple slices

1 package (2 ounces) sweet and sour
  mix
2 green peppers, seeded and cut in
  squares

1. Put pork cubes, onion, and salt in a 2- to 3-quart baking dish or casserole.
2. Cook, covered, on HIGH for 18 to 19 minutes. Stir once.
3. Drain off pork fat.
4. Drain pineapple slices, reserving juice. Add enough water to pineapple juice to make 1¼ cups liquid. Add to pork mixture.
5. Cook, covered, on HIGH for 8 minutes, stirring once during cooking period.
6. Stir in sweet and sour mix. Cook, covered, on HIGH for 8 minutes, stirring once during cooking period.
7. Cut pineapple slices in small pieces. Add to pork mixture with green pepper squares. Cook, covered, on HIGH for 4 minutes, stirring once during cooking period.
8. Remove from oven and let stand 5 minutes.
9. Serve with hot cooked rice or chow mein noodles.

Note: This dish tastes better when it is made early in the day and then heated at dinner time.

Barbecued Spareribs
4 servings

 2 tablespoons cooking oil
½ cup minced onions
 2 cans (8 ounces each) tomato sauce
 2 tablespoons lemon juice
 2 tablespoons brown sugar
 1 tablespoon white sugar

2 teaspoons Worcestershire sauce
1 teaspoon prepared mustard
1 teaspoon salt
¼ teaspoon black pepper
1½ pounds spareribs

1. Put oil and onion in a 1-quart casserole. Cook, covered, on HIGH for 3 to 4 minutes.
2. Add 2 tablespoons of water and remaining ingredients except spareribs. Cover and cook on HIGH for 3 minutes.
3. Cover and let stand.
4. Cut ribs apart between bones and place in a 3-quart casserole.
5. Cook, covered, on ROAST for 26 minutes.
6. Pour off fat and juices. Cover ribs with ¾ cup of the barbecue sauce mixture.
7. Cook, uncovered, on ROAST for 15 minutes.
8. Turn ribs over. Spoon sauce over top. Cook on ROAST for 10 minutes, or until meat is tender.
9. Stir sauce and cook again for 8 minutes, stirring after 5 minutes.
10. Let stand a few minutes before serving.

Note: This recipe makes about 2½ cups sauce. Save remainder for other ribs or use on chicken or barbecued steak.

Baked Ham

10 to 12 servings

½ precooked smoked ham,
about 4 pounds
1 can (4 ounces) pineapple slices,
drained, juice reserved

¼ cup brown sugar
10 to 12 whole cloves

1. Place ham, fat side down, on a rack or inverted saucer in a baking dish.
2. Cook, covered with plastic wrap, on ROAST for 20 minutes.
3. Remove ham from oven. Turn fat side up. Combine 2 tablespoons of the pineapple juice with the brown sugar to make a sauce. Put pineapple slices on top of ham. Stud with cloves. Drizzle pineapple juice mixture over top of ham.
4. Cook, uncovered, 15 to 20 minutes, or until ham is heated through.
5. Cover with a tent of aluminum foil and let stand about 20 minutes before carving.

Baked Ham Steak

2 servings

1 precooked ham steak, about 1
pound

2 teaspoons brown sugar
½ teaspoon prepared mustard

1. Put ham steak in an 8-inch square baking dish.
2. Cook, covered, on ROAST for 4 minutes.
3. Remove from oven and drain off juices. Mix juices with brown sugar and mustard. Spread over top of steak.
4. Cook, uncovered, on ROAST for 2 minutes.
5. Cover loosely and let stand 2 or 3 minutes before serving.

Scalloped Potatoes and Ham

4 servings

1½ cups milk
2 cups leftover pieces of baked ham
4 cups sliced potatoes
⅔ cup chopped onions
2 tablespoons all-purpose flour

1 teaspoon salt
⅛ teaspoon pepper
2 tablespoons butter or margarine
Paprika

1. Put milk in a 2-cup measure.
2. Cook, covered with waxed paper, on HIGH for 2 to 3 minutes, or just long enough to warm milk.
3. Put a layer of ham in bottom of a 3-quart glass casserole. Add a layer of potatoes and onions. Sprinkle with flour, salt, and pepper. Dot with butter. Add another layer of ham, potatoes, and onions. Pour warm milk over layers. Sprinkle with paprika.
4. Cook, covered, on HIGH for 10 minutes.
5. Cook, uncovered, on ROAST for 15 minutes, or until potatoes are tender.
6. Cover loosely with plastic wrap and let stand 2 minutes before serving.

Ham Casserole

4 servings

1½ cups diced cooked ham
2 tablespoons chopped onion
⅛ teaspoon tarragon
2 tablespoons butter or margarine
1 can (10½ ounces) condensed cream of chicken soup, undiluted

1½ cups cooked narrow egg noodles
½ cup cooked French-style green beans
2 tablespoons buttered bread crumbs

1. Combine ham, onion, tarragon, and butter in a 1½-quart casserole.
2. Cook, covered, on HIGH for 3 minutes.
3. Add chicken soup, egg noodles, green beans, and ½ cup water. Toss lightly.
4. Cook, covered, on HIGH for 5 minutes, or until piping hot. Stir once during cooking period.
5. Top with crumbs. Cover and let stand 2 to 3 minutes.

Bacon

8 strips

8 slices bacon

1. Separate bacon strips and lay 4 slices in an oblong baking dish on 2 layers of paper towels. Cover with 1 piece of paper towel. Place 4 more slices bacon on towel. Cover with towel.
2. Cook on HIGH for 6 to 8 minutes, or to the desired degree of crispness.

Note: Cooking bacon in the microwave oven has more variables than almost any other food. Cooking time depends on the thickness of the slice, the amount of fat in the bacon, and the desired degree of crispness. It may be advisable to cook it the first time at the times suggested here, and thereafter cook it according to your own findings.

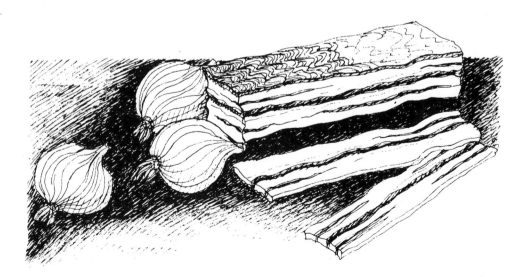

Poultry

Frozen whole chickens and turkeys can be successfully thawed in the microwave oven—just make sure to rotate the bird often. Allow the fowl to rest in between periods in the oven. Cover spots that begin to cook with bits of aluminum foil so that when the bird is cooked you will not have overdone spots. When roasting a bird, check for doneness by removing the bird from the oven and inserting the thermometer. If the temperature is 20° below the final temperature desired, it is time to let the bird stand—it will finish cooking out of the oven.

When cooking chicken parts, put the larger pieces of chicken on the outer edges of the dish and the smaller pieces in the center, so that all pieces will cook evenly.

Roast Chicken with Stuffing

4 to 6 servings

1 roasting chicken, about 5 pounds
½ package (7 ounces) stuffing mix

Salt to taste
Butter

1. Wash chicken. Reserve giblets and neck and use for chicken stock.
2. Prepare stuffing mix according to package directions.
3. Sprinkle inside of cavity with salt. Fill cavity and neck opening with stuffing. Secure with toothpicks. Tie legs together loosely. Tie wings to body with string. Cover ends of the legs, the tail, and the wings with small pieces of aluminum foil.
4. Place inverted saucers in a 2-quart oblong baking dish. Place chicken breast-side down on saucers. Brush with butter. Cook, uncovered, on HIGH for 20 minutes.
5. Remove chicken from dish and turn over so that breast side is up. Remove pieces of foil from chicken. Brush with butter. Cover with a piece of waxed paper. Insert microwave oven meat thermometer in breast of chicken so that it does not touch the bone.
6. Cook about 20 to 30 minutes, or until the meat thermometer registers 170° F.
7. Cover loosely with foil and let stand 10 to 15 minutes before carving. During this time the thermometer will rise to 185° F on microwave oven thermometer. The standard meat thermometer is marked off for degree of doneness for chicken.

COOKING TIME FOR ROAST CHICKEN

Cooking time on HIGH is about 9 minutes per pound.

General Method:
Compute time before starting to cook. Cook the chicken breast-side down for half the time, then invert the chicken and cook for the remaining time breast-side up.

Chicken Balkan

4 servings

½ cup butter or margarine
1 broiler-fryer chicken, cut in serving pieces
1 onion, sliced
⅓ cup dry sherry

½ cup tomato juice
1 teaspoon paprika
1 teaspoon salt
Freshly ground pepper to taste

1. Place butter in an 8-inch square baking dish. Cook, uncovered, on ROAST for about 1 minute to 1½ minutes, or just until butter melts.
2. Cut large pieces of chicken in half. Put in baking dish and turn so that all pieces are coated with melted butter. Place breasts in center of dish and surround with remaining pieces of chicken. Sprinkle onion slices on top.

3. Cook, uncovered, on HIGH for 5 minutes.
4. Combine remaining ingredients with ½ cup water. Pour over chicken.
5. Cook, covered, on HIGH for 23 to 25 minutes, or until chicken is tender.
6. Serve with rice pilaf.

Chicken Cacciatore   4 servings

¼ cup cooking oil	1¼ teaspoons salt
1 broiler-fryer chicken, cut in serving pieces	⅛ teaspoon pepper
	½ bay leaf
1 medium onion, coarsely chopped	1 can (16 ounces) tomatoes
1 clove garlic, minced	2 tablespoons dry white wine
1 medium green pepper, seeded and coarsely chopped	Chopped parsley

1. Pour oil into an 8-inch square baking dish. Cut large pieces of chicken in half. Put in baking dish and turn so that all pieces are coated with oil. Place breasts in center and surround with other pieces of chicken. Sprinkle onion and garlic on top of chicken. Cook on HIGH for 5 minutes.
2. Combine green pepper, salt, pepper, bay leaf, tomatoes, and wine. Stir with a fork and mash tomatoes into small pieces. Pour over top of chicken.
3. Cook, covered, on HIGH for 23 to 25 minutes, or until chicken is tender.
4. Garnish with parsley and serve with cooked spaghetti.

Bacon-Flake Chicken   4 to 6 servings

5 slices bacon, cut in half	2 cups crushed corn flakes
3 whole chicken breasts	Salt and pepper
1 cup milk	Garlic salt

1. Put bacon in a shallow 8- by 10-inch baking dish. Cover with waxed paper and cook on HIGH for 5 minutes.
2. Turn bacon over. Cook on HIGH for 3 minutes, or until very crisp.
3. Cut chicken breasts in half. Remove skin and breastbone. Dip chicken in milk and roll in corn flakes. Pat corn flakes on so that they stick all over chicken. Place on top of cooked bacon. Pour remaining milk carefully into dish without disturbing chicken.
4. Cook, uncovered, on HIGH for 5 minutes.
5. Turn chicken over. Sprinkle with salt and pepper. Cook on BAKE for 8 minutes. Let stand 3 minutes before serving. Sprinkle with garlic salt just before serving.

FOLLOWING PAGES: Left, *Chicken Cacciatore, page 63;* right, *Turkey Divan, page 67.*

Roast Turkey

1. Select a turkey between 8 and 12 pounds. A large bird can be cooked in the oven if you can easily get it in and out of the oven when it is raised on saucers out of the drippings or placed on a microwave roast rack. A smaller bird is easier to maneuver and will not require any forcing.
2. Remove giblets and neck from turkey and rinse body cavity with water. Cook giblets and neck on top of the range in a conventional manner and use the broth for gravy or soup.
3. Pat turkey dry with paper towels. If stuffing is desired, stuff main cavity and neck cavity with desired stuffing. Secure neck skin and body opening with skewers. Tie wings to body loosely with string. Tie legs together loosely. Cover wings and legs with small pieces of foil.
4. Place inverted saucers or a microwave roast rack in the bottom of a 2- or 3-quart baking dish, depending on the size of the turkey. Turkey should not extend over sides of dish. Place turkey breast-side down.
5. Cook, uncovered, on HIGH for half the allotted cooking time. (Compute time from the following table before you start cooking.) Remove turkey and turn breast-side up. Remove foil pieces. Brush with melted butter.
6. Insert a microwave meat thermometer into thickest part of breast or thigh of turkey or cook, uncovered, on HIGH for the last half of the allotted cooking time. If the bird develops brown spots, this indicates overcooking. These spots may be covered with small pieces of aluminum foil to prevent further overcooking.
7. When microwave meat thermometer reaches 170° F, remove turkey. If you do not have a microwave oven thermometer, use a regular meat thermometer when the turkey is out of the oven. The thermometer should register 170° F when the turkey is removed from the oven, and it will climb to 185° F as the turkey stands. Cover turkey with foil and let stand about 20 minutes to bring it up to temperature and to make it easier to carve.

COOKING TIME FOR TURKEY

8 to 9 minutes per pound.
Do not use the regular meat thermometer in the microwave oven while cooking. Insert the thermometer when the turkey is taken from the oven. If turkey requires additional cooking time, remove thermometer and reinsert when turkey is removed from the oven for the second time.

Turkey Tetrazzini

6 servings

4 ounces thin spaghetti
3 tablespoons butter or margarine
1 can (4 ounces) sliced mushrooms, drained
⅓ cup finely minced onions
3 tablespoons all-purpose flour
2 cups chicken broth or milk

½ cup light cream
¼ cup dry vermouth
1 teaspoon salt
Dash of white pepper
¾ cup grated Parmesan cheese, divided
2 cups diced cooked turkey

1. Cook spaghetti according to package directions. Drain immediately and rinse in cold water to stop cooking. Reserve.
2. Place butter in a 3-quart casserole. Add mushrooms and onion.
3. Cook, covered, on SAUTE for 3 to 4 minutes, or until onions are soft.
4. Add flour and mix to form a smooth paste.
5. Cook, covered, on HIGH for 30 seconds.
6. Stir in chicken broth, cream, vermouth, salt, pepper, and ¼ cup Parmesan cheese. Blend well.
7. Cook, uncovered, on HIGH for 4 to 5 minutes, or until mixture comes to a boil and thickens. Stir once during cooking period.
8. Add cooked spaghetti, turkey, and remainder of cheese. Toss slightly.
9. Cook, covered, on BAKE for 8 to 9 minutes, or until piping hot.
10. Let stand on WARM for 5 minutes before serving.

Note: Chicken or ham may be substituted for the turkey.

Turkey Divan

4 to 6 servings

1 bunch broccoli, cooked
8 to 12 slices cooked turkey breast
2 cups white sauce (see page 108)

¼ cup grated Parmesan cheese
¼ cup grated Gruyere cheese

1. Place cooked broccoli in a baking dish with flower ends at ends of dish. Cover center of stalks with slices of cooked turkey.
2. Prepare white sauce, and while it is still warm add the cheeses. Stir until well blended. Pour over top of turkey. Sprinkle with additional Parmesan cheese if desired.
3. Cook, covered, on BAKE for 9 to 10 minutes, or until turkey is piping hot.

Fish

Cooking fish in the microwave oven is one of the greatest time- and flavor-savers. Fish virtually cooks itself—the only trick is to be sure that it is not overcooked. Cook just until the fish flakes easily when tested with a fork—this can be done often during cooking time. Then remove from the oven and let stand for a time, because it continues to cook while standing. Shellfish should be watched even more carefully because it toughens very rapidly if over-cooked.

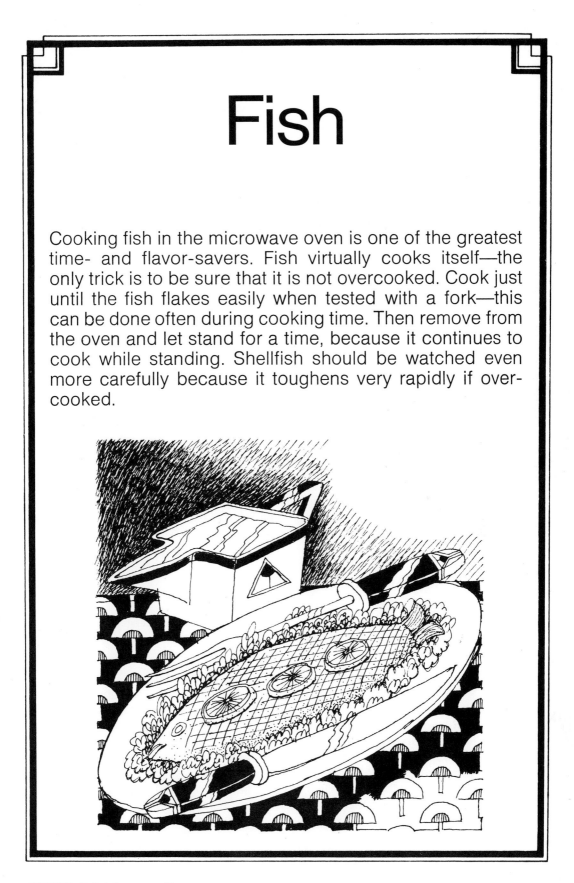

OPPOSITE: *Stuffed Bass, page 70.*

Stuffed Bass

4 to 6 servings

1 whole bass, cleaned, about 3 pounds
2 cups fresh bread cubes
1 tablespoon melted butter or margarine
Salt and pepper to taste

1 tablespoon chopped parsley
1 teaspoon lemon juice
3 slices bacon

1. Wash fish in cold water. Pat dry with paper towels.
2. Combine bread cubes, butter, salt and pepper, parsley, and lemon juice. Toss lightly. Stuff cavity of fish. Close with toothpicks or tie with string.
3. Place fish in an oblong baking dish. Place bacon slices on fish.
4. Cook, covered, on HIGH for 16 to 18 minutes, or until fish flakes easily when tested with a fork.
5. Let fish stand covered with paper towels 5 minutes before serving.

Halibut Steaks

4 servings

2 halibut steaks, about ¾ inch thick
½ lemon
1 egg, beaten
½ can (10¾ ounces) condensed cream of celery soup

2 tablespoons milk
2 tablespoons grated Parmesan cheese, divided
2 tablespoons fine dry bread crumbs
2 teaspoons melted butter or margarine

1. Wipe fish with a damp paper towel. Cut each steak in 2 portions. Place in an 8-inch square baking dish. Squeeze lemon over top of fish. Set aside.
2. In a 2-cup measure beat together egg, soup, milk, and 1 tablespoon cheese.
3. Cook, covered, on ROAST for 2 minutes. Remove and stir well to melt cheese.
4. Pour soup mixture over steaks. Combine bread crumbs and melted butter and sprinkle over top of fish. Top with remaining 1 tablespoon cheese.
5. Cook, covered, on HIGH for 6 minutes, or until fish flakes when tested with a fork.

Fillet of Sole Almondine

4 servings

½ cup slivered almonds
½ cup butter or margarine
1 pound fresh or frozen fillet of sole
½ teaspoon salt

⅛ teaspoon pepper
1 teaspoon chopped parsley
1 tablespoon lemon juice

1. Place almonds and butter in an 8-inch square baking dish.
2. Cook, uncovered, on HIGH for 5 minutes, or until almonds and butter are golden brown. Remove almonds with a slotted spoon and set aside.
3. Arrange sole in dish with butter, turning to coat both sides of fish. Sprinkle with salt, pepper, parsley, and lemon juice.
4. Cook, covered with waxed paper, on HIGH for 4 minutes.
5. Remove waxed paper. Sprinkle fish with toasted almonds. Cook, covered, on HIGH for 2 minutes, or until fish flakes easily when tested with a fork.
6. Let stand 1 to 2 minutes before serving. To serve, garnish with lemon wedges and sprigs of parsley.

Tuna-Spinach Casserole

4 servings

1 package (10 ounces) raw spinach
1 can (7 ounces) solid pack tuna
1 can (4 ounces) sliced mushrooms
2 tablespoons lemon juice
3 tablespoons butter or margarine, divided

1 tablespoon minced onion
2 tablespoons all-purpose flour
½ teaspoon salt
⅛ teaspoon pepper
1 egg, lightly beaten

1. Rinse spinach in fresh, cold water. Drain well. Break in pieces, removing tough center stems. Put in a 2-quart casserole.
2. Cook, covered, on HIGH for 3 to 4 minutes, or until spinach is limp. Drain well and set aside.
3. Drain tuna and set aside.
4. Drain mushrooms, reserving liquid. Put mushroom liquid in a 1-cup measure. Add lemon juice and enough water to make 1 cup of liquid.
5. Put 2 tablespoons of the butter in a 1-quart casserole. Cook on HIGH for 30 seconds, or just long enough to melt butter.
6. Add onion, flour, salt, and pepper. Cook, uncovered, on BAKE for 1 minute.
7. Stir in mushroom liquid. Cook, uncovered, on BAKE for 5 minutes, or until thick, stirring occasionally during cooking time.
8. Add a small amount of sauce to egg, beat well, and return to hot sauce. Stir mushrooms into sauce.
9. Put drained spinach in a 2- to 3-quart casserole. Break tuna in big chunks and place over top of spinach. Pour sauce over top. Dot with remaining 1 tablespoon of butter.
10. Cook, uncovered, on HIGH for 4 minutes. Let stand covered with waxed paper 3 to 5 minutes before serving.

Steamed Clams

2 servings

1 quart steamer clams   Melted butter or margarine

1. Scrub clams with a stiff brush to remove all sand and grit. Discard all clams that are even the least bit open.
2. Put scrubbed clams in a 2-quart casserole. Add 2 tablespoons water.
3. Cook, covered, on HIGH for 8 minutes, or until clam shells are open and clams are cooked. Discard clams with closed shells.
4. Serve clams in flat bowls. Divide clam liquid into custard cups and fill a second set of cups with melted butter. Remove clams from shells, dip in clam liquid, and then in butter.
5. Drink clam broth when clams have been eaten.

FOLLOWING PAGES: Left, *Filet of Sole Almondine, page 70;* right, *Tuna Crunch, page 74.*

Tuna Crunch

4 servings

1 cup thinly sliced celery
¼ cup chopped onion
2 tablespoons butter or margarine
1 can (7 ounces) tuna fish

1 can (10¾ ounces) cream of
   mushroom soup, undiluted
1 can (3 ounces) chow mein noodles
½ cup coarsely chopped cashews

1. Combine celery, onion, and butter in a 1-quart casserole. Cook, uncovered, on HIGH for 5 minutes, stirring once during cooking time.
2. Drain tuna and flake with a fork. Add to onion mixture with soup, ⅔ can of noodles, and cashews. Toss lightly.
3. Cook, covered, on HIGH for 2 minutes.
4. Stir mixture lightly. Top with remaining noodles. Cook, covered, on HIGH for 3 to 4 minutes, or until piping hot.

Crab Meat in Shells

4 servings

1 tablespoon chopped parsley
1 tablespoon chopped green pepper
1 scallion, chopped, including green
   top
1 can (4 ounces) sliced mushrooms and
   pieces, well drained
1 teaspoon butter
1 can (10¾ ounces) condensed cream
   of celery soup, undiluted

1 can (7½ ounces) crab meat
1 tablespoon lemon juice
1 tablespoon dry sherry
2 tablespoons dry bread crumbs
2 tablespoons grated Cheddar cheese
Paprika

1. Combine parsley, green pepper, scallion, mushrooms, and butter in a 1-quart casserole.
2. Cook, covered, on HIGH for 3 minutes.
3. Add soup and blend well. Cook, covered, on HIGH for 1 minute.
4. Pick over crab meat and remove any bits of cartilage. Add to mixture with lemon juice and sherry. Divide mixture into 4 scallop shells. Combine bread crumbs and cheese. Spread over top of crab mixture. Sprinkle generously with paprika.
5. Cook two shells at a time on HIGH for 3 minutes, or until piping hot.

Lobster Tails

4 servings

1 pound frozen lobster tails
1 teaspoon lemon juice

¼ cup butter or margarine
¼ teaspoon grated lemon peel

1. Place frozen lobster tails in an 8-inch square baking dish. Sprinkle with lemon juice. Cook on HIGH for 4 minutes to thaw lobster.
2. Cut away soft shell-like surface on underside of tail with a sharp knife or scissors. Insert wooden skewers into each lobster tail to keep flat while cooking. Drain liquid from dish and arrange lobster in dish shell side down. down.

3. Combine butter and lemon peel in a small custard cup. Cook on ROAST for 30 seconds, or until butter is melted.
4. Brush tails with butter mixture.
5. Cook, covered, on HIGH for 7 minutes, or until lobster meat turns pink.
6. Serve hot with melted butter and lemon wedges.

Scallops Poulette   4 servings

¼ cup butter or margarine	⅛ teaspoon pepper
1 tablespoon minced onion	1 pound bay scallops
2 tablespoons flour	1 bay leaf
1 can (4 ounces) sliced mushrooms, drained	2 teaspoons lemon juice
¼ cup dry vermouth	½ cup light cream
½ teaspoon salt	1 egg yolk
	1 tablespoon chopped parsley

1. Combine butter and onion in a 2-quart casserole.
2. Cook, uncovered, on HIGH for 2 minutes.
3. Stir in flour and blend well. Add mushrooms, wine, salt, pepper, scallops, bay leaf, and lemon juice. Toss together lightly.
4. Cook, covered, on HIGH for 6 minutes, or until scallops are tender.
5. Remove bay leaf. Beat together cream and egg yolk. Add some hot liquid carefully to egg and blend well. Stir egg mixture carefully into hot casserole. Stir well.
6. Cook, covered, on BAKE for 5 minutes, stirring once during cooking period.
7. Sprinkle with parsley and serve.

Shrimp Creole   6 servings

3 tablespoons butter or margarine	1 tablespoon Worcestershire sauce
½ cup chopped onions	1½ teaspoons salt
½ cup chopped green pepper	1 teaspoon sugar
½ cup diced celery	½ teaspoon chili powder
1 clove garlic, minced	Dash of hot-pepper sauce
1 can (1 pound) tomatoes, mashed	1 tablespoon cornstarch
1 can (8 ounces) tomato sauce	1 pound cooked shrimp

1. Combine butter, onion, green pepper, celery, and garlic in a 2- or 3-quart casserole.
2. Cook, uncovered, on HIGH for 3 minutes.
3. Add tomatoes, tomato sauce, Worcestershire, salt, sugar, chili powder, and hot-pepper sauce.
4. Cook, uncovered, on HIGH for 7 minutes, stirring once.
5. Combine cornstarch with 2 teaspoons cold water. Stir into casserole.
6. Cook, uncovered, on HIGH for 3 minutes, stirring once.
7. Add shrimp. Cook, uncovered, on HIGH for 2 minutes, or until shrimp is piping hot.
8. Serve with wild rice or plain boiled rice.

FOLLOWING PAGES: Left, *Steamed Clams, page 71;* right, *Shrimp Creole, page 75.*

Scallops Cacciatore

4 servings

1 medium onion, chopped
1 medium green pepper, chopped
¼ cup salad oil
1 can (1 pound) tomatoes, drained
1 pound bay scallops
1 can (8 ounces) tomato sauce

¼ cup dry white wine
1¼ teaspoons salt
⅛ teaspoon pepper
2 bay leaves
2 tablespoons chopped parsley

1. Combine onion, green pepper, and oil in a 1½- to 2-quart casserole.
2. Cook, covered, on HIGH for 3 minutes, stirring once.
3. Mash tomatoes with a fork to break into small pieces. Add to casserole with scallops, tomato sauce, wine, salt, pepper, and bay leaves.
4. Cook, covered, on HIGH for 6 minutes, or until scallops are tender.
5. Sprinkle with parsley. Serve with hot cooked rice, if desired.

Eggs, Pasta, and Cheese

Eggs and cheese require careful watching and cooking. Eggs cook so quickly that they can easily be overcooked in just seconds. Time them carefully. When baking or shirring eggs, it is wise to prick the yolk gently with the point of a very sharp knife—just enough to allow the steam to escape so that the yolks will not burst. Cheese that is overcooked by any method—conventional or microwave —will become rubbery. Undercook slightly, rather than overcook any cheese dish.

FOLLOWING PAGES: Left, *Eggs Benedict, page 82;* right, *Shirred Eggs, page 82; Sticky Buns, page 138.*

Poached Egg   1 serving

1 egg

1. Put ½ cup water into a custard cup. Cook on HIGH for 2 minutes, or until water boils.
2. Carefully break egg into a small dish or saucer. Slide egg into boiling water.
3. Cook, tightly covered, on SIMMER for 1 minute. Keep covered and let stand 1 minute before serving.

Fried Egg   1 serving

1 teaspoon butter or margarine   **1 egg**

1. Place butter in a small custard cup or sauce dish. Cook on ROAST for 30 seconds, or just until melted.
2. Carefully break egg into dish. Cook, tightly covered, on ROAST for 1¼ minutes. Keep covered and let stand 1 minute before serving.

Eggs Benedict   4 servings

¾ cup hollandaise sauce   **4 slices ham, ¼ to ½ inch thick**
2 English muffins, split and toasted   **4 poached eggs**

1. Prepare hollandaise sauce. Cover with a piece of waxed paper and set aside.
2. Place each muffin half on a paper plate and top each with 1 slice ham.
3. Cook, uncovered, 2 at a time, on ROAST for 2 to 2½ minutes, or until ham is hot.
4. Top each with a poached egg. Cover with hollandaise sauce and serve immediately.

Shirred Eggs   1 serving

1 teaspoon butter or margarine   **1 tablespoon cream**
2 eggs

1. Melt butter in a ramekin or small cereal bowl on ROAST for 30 seconds.
2. Break eggs carefully into ramekin or bowl. Add cream. Cover tightly with plastic wrap.
3. Cook, covered, on BAKE for 2 to 2½ minutes.
4. Remove and let stand 1 minute before serving.

Welsh Rabbit on Toast   4 to 6 servings

4 teaspoons butter or margarine   **¼ teaspoon dry mustard**
4 cups (1 pound) shredded sharp   **¼ teaspoon cayenne**
  Cheddar cheese   **2 eggs, lightly beaten**
¾ teaspoon Worcestershire sauce   **1 cup flat beer or ale, at room**
½ teaspoon salt   **temperature**
½ teaspoon paprika

1. Melt butter in a 2-quart casserole or bowl on BAKE for 2 minutes.
2. Add cheese, Worcestershire, salt, paprika, dry mustard, and cayenne. Mix thoroughly.
3. Cook, covered, on SIMMER for 6 minutes, stirring once during cooking time.
4. Stir a little of the hot cheese into beaten eggs. Return slowly to hot mixture and stir briskly. Gradually stir in beer and blend well.
5. Cook, covered, on SIMMER for 3 minutes. Remove from oven and stir well.
6. Cook, covered, on SIMMER for 3 minutes. Remove from oven and beat briskly with a whisk to blend thoroughly.
7. Serve over crisp toasted French bread slices and garnish with tomatoes and crisp bacon slices.

Swiss Cheese Fondue   6 servings

4 cups shredded Swiss cheese	**Dash of pepper**
¼ cup all-purpose flour	**2 cups dry white wine**
¼ teaspoon salt	**2 tablespoons Kirsch**
¼ teaspoon nutmeg	**1 loaf French bread, cut into cubes**

1. In a 1½-quart dish or casserole combine cheese, flour, salt, nutmeg, and pepper. Toss lightly to coat cheese with flour. Stir in wine.
2. Cook, covered, on SIMMER for 6 minutes, stirring three times during cooking time. Stir well after removing from oven to finish melting cheese.
3. If cheese is not all melted, cook, covered, on SIMMER for 1 minute.
4. Stir in Kirsch.
5. Serve immediately with cubes of French bread. Spear each cube of bread on a fondue fork; dip into fondue and eat immediately.
6. If fondue cools during eating time, rewarm on SIMMER for 1 to 2 minutes.

Green Noodles   6 servings

¼ cup butter or margarine	**1 cup diced sharp Cheddar cheese**
¼ cup all-purpose flour	**¼ cup grated Parmesan cheese**
1 teaspoon salt	**3 cups cooked green noodles**
¼ teaspoon hot-pepper sauce	**3 hard-cooked eggs, halved**
2½ cups milk	

1. Put butter in a 1-quart measure.
2. Cook, covered, on HIGH for 30 seconds.
3. Remove and stir in flour, salt, and hot-pepper sauce to make a smooth paste.
4. Cook on HIGH for 30 seconds.
5. Gradually stir in milk. Cook, covered, on HIGH for 4 to 5 minutes, stirring once during cooking time.
6. Remove and stir briskly to make a smooth sauce. Add Cheddar cheese and Parmesan cheese and stir until cheese is melted.
7. Put noodles in a 1½-quart casserole. Add cheese sauce and mix lightly. Cook, covered, on BAKE for 7 to 8 minutes, or until piping hot.
8. Top with egg halves. Cook, covered, on BAKE for 3 minutes.
9. Let stand, covered, for 4 minutes before serving.

FOLLOWING PAGES: Left, *Welsh Rabbit, page 82;* right, *Swiss Cheese Fondue, page 83.*

Manicotti

8 to 10 servings

1 package (8 ounces) manicotti
noodles
1 package (1 pound) ricotta cheese
½ pound mozzarella cheese, grated
Parmesan cheese
3 tablespoons chopped parsley,
divided
3 teaspoons sugar, divided
1 egg, lightly beaten

Salt and pepper to taste
2 sweet Italian sausages
1 clove garlic, minced
1 medium onion, minced
1 pound ground beef
1 can (12 ounces) tomatoes, mashed
1 can (16 ounces) tomato sauce
½ teaspoon basil

1. Cook manicotti noodles according to package directions for 12 minutes on conventional range. Drain and reserve.
2. Combine ricotta, mozzarella, 3 tablespoons Parmesan cheese, 1 tablespoon parsley, 2 teaspoons sugar, egg, and salt and pepper to taste. Blend well and reserve.
3. Remove sausage from casings. Crumble into a 3-quart casserole. Add garlic, onion, and 2 tablespoons chopped parsley.
4. Cook, covered, on HIGH for 3 minutes, stirring once.
5. Crumble ground beef on top of sausage meat and toss lightly. Cook, covered, on HIGH for 5 minutes, stirring once to break up meat during cooking period.
6. Add tomatoes, tomato sauce, basil, 1 teaspoon sugar, and salt and pepper to taste.
7. Cook, covered, on HIGH, stirring once.
8. Pour a thin layer of meat sauce on the bottom of two 2-quart baking dishes or flat casseroles.
9. Fill cooked manicotti tubes with cheese mixture. Place 10 filled tubes close together in each casserole. Cover with remaining meat sauce.
10. Cook, covered tightly, on HIGH for 20 minutes, or until hot.
11. Remove cover, and sprinkle ¼ cup grated Parmesan on top of casserole. Cook on ROAST for 2 minutes, or just until cheese is melted.

Note: This recipe makes 2 casseroles. Use one immediately and freeze the second for later use.

Macaroni Goulash

6 to 8 servings

1 cup uncooked macaroni
1 pound ground beef
1 can (1 pound) tomato puree, or 1 can
(1 pound) tomatoes packed in puree
½ teaspoon sugar

½ teaspoon basil
1 teaspoon salt
Pepper to taste
1 tablespoon chopped parsley

1. Cook macaroni on conventional range according to package directions. Set aside.

2. Crumble beef into a 3-quart casserole. Cook, uncovered, on HIGH for 4 to 5 minutes, stirring once to break up meat.
3. Add puree, sugar, basil, salt, pepper to taste, and parsley. Stir in macaroni.
4. Cook, covered, on HIGH for 8 minutes, stirring once.
5. Cook, covered, on LOW for 4 to 5 minutes before serving.

Variation: To stretch amount, use 1 can (1 pound 12 ounces) tomato puree and increase macaroni to 1½ cups.

Noodles and Chicken   4 to 6 servings

1½ cups broken narrow egg noddles
  2 to 3 cups cut-up cooked chicken or turkey
  1 cup chicken stock
½ cup milk

½ teaspoon salt
⅛ teaspoon pepper
  1 cup shredded Cheddar cheese
¼ cup sliced stuffed green olives

1. In a 2-quart casserole combine noodles, chicken, chicken stock, milk, salt, and pepper. Stir lightly.
2. Cook, covered, on HIGH for 8 to 10 minutes, stirring once, or until noodles are tender.
3. Stir in cheese and olives. Cook, covered, on LOW for 5 minutes, or until cheese is melted.

Sunday-Night Special   4 to 6 servings

1 can (7 ounces) green chilies
1 cup coarsely crushed corn chips
Meat (optional)
  2 mild Italian sausages, cooked and broken up, or
  ½ pound ground chuck, cooked, or
  1 cup ground cooked pork or ham
½ cup cottage cheese or ricotta

4 ounces Monterey Jack cheese, cut in strips
2 eggs
1 cup milk
½ teaspoon salt
½ cup grated Cheddar or Parmesan cheese

1. Wash and dry chilies. Remove any remaining seeds. Cut into strips 1 inch wide.
2. Put half the corn chips in bottom of an 8-inch round cake pan. Arrange about one-third of the chilies on top of corn chips. Place meat, if desired, on top of chilies. Dot cottage cheese on top of meat. Add another third of the chilies. Arrange Monterey Jack cheese over top of chilies. Arrange remaining chilies on top of cheese.
3. Beat together eggs, milk, and salt. Pour over top of mixture in casserole. Sprinkle top with Cheddar or Parmesan cheese. Sprinkle remaining corn chips on top of cheese.
4. Cook, uncovered, on BAKE for 16 to 18 minutes, or until custard is set.
5. Cook, covered, on LOW for 5 minutes.

FOLLOWING PAGES: Left, *Spaghetti Sauce;* right, *Macaroni and Cheese;* page 91.

Swiss and Onion Pie

6 to 8 slices

4 slices bacon	1 tablespoon all-purpose flour
1 large onion, thinly sliced	3 eggs, lightly beaten
1 tablespoon butter or margarine	1 cup milk
1 9-inch baked pastry shell	½ teaspoon salt
½ pound Swiss cheese, grated	⅛ teaspoon pepper

1. Place bacon slices on 2 paper towels. Cover with another paper towel. Cook on BAKE for 5 to 6 minutes, or until almost crisp. Reserve bacon.
2. Combine onion and butter in a 1-quart casserole.
3. Cook, covered, on HIGH for 3 to 4 minutes, or until onion is limp.
4. Place cooked onion in prebaked pastry shell. Toss together cheese and flour and sprinkle over onion. Beat together eggs, milk, salt, and pepper. Pour over cheese.
5. Cook on BAKE for 7 to 8 minutes.
6. Place bacon strips on top of pie. Cook on BAKE for 4 to 5 minutes, or until custard is almost set. Let stand 10 minutes to finish cooking.

Cheese Soufflé

4 to 6 servings

3 tablespoons butter or margarine	1 cup milk
¼ cup all-purpose flour	1½ cups grated sharp Cheddar
½ teaspoon salt	cheese
Grind of fresh pepper	4 eggs, separated

1. Melt butter in a 1-quart glass measure on HIGH for 3 to 4 minutes. Remove from oven and stir in flour, salt, and pepper. Stir in milk and blend until smooth.
2. Cook on HIGH for 2 to 3 minutes, stirring frequently. Remove from oven and beat until smooth. Add cheese and beat until cheese is melted and sauce is smooth.
3. Beat egg whites until stiff but not dry. Set aside.
4. Beat egg yolks. Beat in cheese sauce and stir until sauce is smooth. Fold cheese mixture carefully into egg whites. Pour into a 1½-quart soufflé dish.
5. Cook on BRAISE for 15 to 17 minutes. Turn once during cooking time. When top is dry to the touch, remove and serve immediately.

Note: This mixture may be prepared in 2 small casseroles. Heat one for dinner and freeze the other for later use.

Marinara Sauce

2 to 3 servings

1 can (2 pounds 3 ounces) peeled Italian plum tomatoes	2 teaspoons dried basil
½ cup salad oil	1 tablespoon chopped parsley
¼ cup thinly sliced garlic	Salt and freshly ground pepper to taste

1. Empty tomatoes into a bowl. Crush with hands so that there are no whole tomatoes left.
2. Put oil and garlic in a 1½-quart casserole. Cook at HIGH for 3 minutes.
3. Add basil, parsley, and tomatoes. Cover and cook on REHEAT for 10 minutes. Cook on BAKE for 5 minutes.
4. Let stand 5 minutes. Season to taste with salt and pepper and serve over hot cooked spaghetti.

Spaghetti Sauce   about 2 quarts

½ **pound ground beef**	2 **teaspoons salt**
½ **cup chopped onions**	2 **teaspoons oregano**
2 **cloves garlic, minced**	¼ **teaspoon basil**
1 **can (28 ounces) tomatoes**	¼ **teaspoon ground thyme**
2 **cans (6 ounces each) tomato paste**	**Freshly ground pepper to taste**

1. Crumble beef into a 3-quart casserole. Add onion and garlic.
2. Cook, uncovered, on HIGH for 5 minutes, stirring once to break up meat.
3. Add remaining ingredients. Break up whole tomatoes with a fork or potato masher.
4. Cook, covered, on SIMMER for 25 to 30 minutes, or until mixture is well blended and slightly thickened.
5. Cover and let stand about 5 minutes.
6. Serve over hot cooked spaghetti.

Macaroni and Cheese   4 servings

1½ **cups uncooked macaroni**	**Freshly ground pepper to taste**
2 **tablespoons butter or margarine**	1 **cup milk**
2 **tablespoons all-purpose flour**	2 **cups shredded sharp Cheddar**
¼ **teaspoon salt**	**cheese, divided**
½ **teaspoon Worcestershire sauce**	¼ **cup cracker crumbs**
½ **teaspoon prepared mustard**	**Tomato slices (optional)**

1. Cook macaroni on conventional range according to package directions. Drain and set aside.
2. Melt butter in a 1-quart measure on HIGH for 30 seconds.
3. Stir in flour, salt, Worcestershire, mustard, and pepper. Cook, uncovered, on HIGH for 30 seconds.
4. Gradually stir in milk. Cook, uncovered, on HIGH for 4 to 5 minutes, stirring once during cooking period.
5. Stir in 1½ cups shredded cheese and continue stirring until cheese is melted. If cheese is not melted, cook on HIGH for 30 seconds, or just until cheese is melted.
6. Stir cooked macaroni into sauce. Top with remaining cheese and cracker crumbs, and with tomato slices if desired.
7. Cook, uncovered, on BAKE for 5 to 6 minutes, or until macaroni is piping hot.
8. Cook, covered, on LOW for 5 minutes before serving.

Vegetables

Because vegetables are cooked in very little water, in a tightly covered dish, and for a short length of time, they retain more nutrients and, most important, keep their color and flavor better than with conventional cooking. Vegetables should be crisp-cooked, almost Chinese style, because—as most foods do—they will continue to cook after they are removed from the microwave oven. In order to assure even cooking, vegetables should be cut in uniform pieces and stirred during the cooking time.

OPPOSITE: *Harvard Beets, page 99.*

Artichoke Hearts

3 to 4 servings

Place a 10-ounce package frozen artichoke hearts in a 1-quart casserole. Add 2 to 3 tablespoons water. Cook, covered, on HIGH for 4 to 5 minutes, or until artichoke hearts are tender. Stir once during cooking time.

Artichoke Hearts with Mushrooms

3 to 4 servings

1 package (10 ounces) frozen artichoke hearts	½ teaspoon lemon juice
	Salt and pepper
1 can (4 ounces) sliced mushrooms	Onion salt
1½ teaspoons cornstarch	Garlic salt
2 tablespoons dry sherry	1 tablespoon chopped parsley
2 tablespoons butter or margarine	

1. Cook artichoke hearts according to preceding directions. Set aside.
2. Drain mushrooms, reserving liquid.
3. Combine cornstarch, sherry, butter, lemon juice, and mushroom liquid in a 1-quart bowl.
4. Cook, uncovered, on HIGH for 30 seconds to 1 minute, or until mixture is thickened and clear. Blend well.
5. Season to taste with salt, pepper, onion salt, and garlic salt. Stir in parsley. Cut artichoke hearts in half and add them, along with the mushrooms. Stir gently.
6. Heat, covered, on HIGH for 2 to 3 minutes, or until mixture is piping hot.

Asparagus

3 to 4 servings

Buy straight, green, crisp stalks with close, compact heads. Select stalks of uniform size so that they will all cook in the same length of time.

Break off each stalk as far down as it will snap easily. Scrub lightly with a soft brush and remove scales with a knife, or remove scales and thinly pare the stalks with a vegetable peeler. The latter method is recommended if stalks are very thick and tough and if the asparagus is very sandy.

Lay 1 pound asparagus spears in a flat dish. Add ½ cup water. Cook, covered, on HIGH for 6 to 7 minutes, or until asparagus is tender.

Frozen Asparagus

2 to 3 servings

Place a 10-ounce package asparagus spears, icy side up, in a 1-quart casserole. Cook, covered, on HIGH for 8 to 9 minutes.

Asparagus Vinaigrette Bundles

5 to 6 servings

2 dozen fresh asparagus spears
6 tablespoons cooking oil
3 tablespoons vinegar
⅛ teaspoon hot-pepper sauce

½ teaspoon sugar
¼ teaspoon salt
1 small onion, sliced
Pimiento strips

1. Cook asparagus spears 6 to 7 minutes. Cool. Place in a shallow dish.
2. Combine remaining ingredients, except pimiento, and blend well. Pour over asparagus and let stand in refrigerator several hours or overnight.
3. Wrap pimiento strips around 4 or 5 asparagus spears. Serve as a cold vegetable or place on lettuce cups and serve as a salad.

Green Beans

3 to 4 servings

Choose crisp, brightly colored, fully formed pods. Wash beans. Remove ends and cut or break 1 pound beans into pieces of uniform size. Place beans in a 1-quart casserole. Add ⅓ cup water. Cook, covered, on HIGH for 12 to 14 minutes, or until beans are cooked to the desired degree of tenderness.

Frozen Green Beans

2 to 3 servings

Place a 10-ounce package of frozen green beans in a 1-quart casserole. Add 3 tablespoons water. Cook, covered, on HIGH for 7 to 8 minutes, or until tender.

Peppered Beans

3 to 4 servings

1 pound green beans
2 tablespoons olive oil
½ sweet red or green pepper, seeded and cut in slivers

¼ cup blanched slivered almonds
Salt and pepper to taste

1. Cook beans according to preceding directions. Cover and let stand.
2. Combine oil, red or green pepper, and almonds in a 1-quart casserole.
3. Cook, uncovered, on HIGH for 3 to 4 minutes, or until peppers are limp.
4. Toss with green beans. Season to taste with salt and pepper.

Green Beans Italian

6 servings

2 packages (10 ounces each) frozen
green beans
1 small onion, thinly sliced

¾ cup bottled Italian dressing
3 strips cooked bacon

1. Place green beans in a 1½-quart casserole or saucepan, icy side up.
2. Cook, covered, on HIGH for 7 to 8 minutes, or until almost tender, stirring once during cooking time.
3. Add onion and Italian dressing.
4. Cook, covered, on HIGH for 3 to 4 minutes, or until beans are crisply tender.
5. Serve hot, topped with crumbled cooked bacon.

Green Beans Piquant

3 to 4 servings

1 pound green beans
2 tablespoons butter or margarine
1 teaspoon prepared mustard

1 tablespoon Worcestershire sauce
Salt and pepper to taste

1. Cook beans according to directions on page 95.
2. When beans are tender, add remaining ingredients and toss lightly until butter is melted and beans are well coated with mixture.

Savory Green Beans

3 to 4 servings

1 pound green beans
2 tablespoons olive oil
1 clove garlic, minced
1 teaspoon catsup

1 teaspoon Worcestershire sauce
¼ teaspoon savory
Salt to taste

1. Cook green beans according to directions. Cover and keep warm.
2. Combine olive oil and garlic in a 1-quart serving bowl.
3. Cook, uncovered, on HIGH for 1½ minutes, or until garlic is tender.
4. Add catsup, Worcestershire, and savory. Add hot beans and toss lightly. Season to taste with salt.

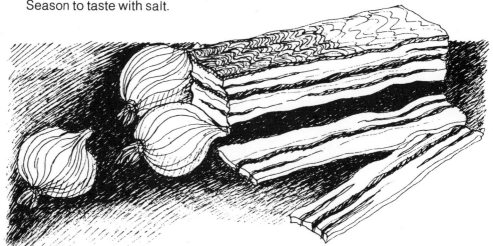

OPPOSITE: *Stuffed Eggplant, Stuffed Green Peppers, page 102; Eggs in Nests, page 103.*

Frozen Lima Beans

3 to 4 servings

Place a 10-ounce package of frozen baby lima beans in a 1-quart casserole. Add ¼ cup water. Cook, covered, on HIGH for 9 to 10 minutes, or until tender. Stir once during cooking time.

Lima Beans Parmesan

3 to 4 servings

1 package (10 ounces) frozen baby lima beans
¼ cup chicken bouillon
1 bay leaf
1 clove garlic
Salt and pepper to taste
Grated Parmesan cheese

1. Place lima beans in a 1½-quart casserole. Add chicken bouillon, bay leaf, and garlic.
2. Cook, covered, on HIGH for 9 to 10 minutes.
3. Remove bay leaf and garlic. Season to taste with salt and pepper. Serve with Parmesan cheese sprinkled on top of beans.

Beets

4 servings

Wash well and cut stems and root ends from 1 bunch (4 to 5 medium-size) beets. Place in a deep 2½-quart mixing bowl with water to cover. Cover with plastic wrap. Cook on HIGH for 18 to 24 minutes, or until beets can be easily pierced with the point of a sharp knife. Drain; slip off skins. Serve whole or sliced with seasoning and butter.

Beets in Orange Sauce

4 servings

1 can (1 pound) diced beets
1 tablespoon cornstarch
¾ teaspoon salt
1½ tablespoons sugar
¼ cup orange juice
2 tablespoons lemon juice
½ teaspoon grated orange peel
1 tablespoon butter or margarine

1. Drain beets, reserving liquid. Pour liquid into a measuring cup and add enough water to make ½ cup liquid.
2. Combine cornstarch, salt, sugar, and orange juice in a 1-quart bowl. Stir in beet liquid.
3. Cook, uncovered, on HIGH for 2½ to 3 minutes, or until mixture comes to a boil and is clear.
4. Add lemon juice, orange peel, and butter. Stir to melt butter. Add beets.
5. Cook, uncovered, on HIGH for about 3 minutes, or until beets are piping hot.

Harvard Beets

4 servings

1 can (1 pound) diced or sliced beets	½ teaspoon salt
¼ cup sugar	Freshly ground pepper to taste
1 tablespoon cornstarch	¼ cup vinegar

1. Drain beets, reserving liquid. Pour beet liquid into a 1-cup measure and add enough water to make 1 cup of liquid.
2. Combine sugar, cornstarch, salt, pepper, and vinegar in a 1-quart casserole or bowl. Stir in beet liquid.
3. Cook, uncovered, on HIGH for 2½ to 3 minutes, stirring occasionally, until mixture thickens and is clear.
4. Add beets and stir lightly.
5. Cook, covered, on HIGH for about 3 minutes, or until beets are piping hot.

Pickled Beets

2 cups

1 can (1 pound) sliced beets	⅓ cup vinegar
⅓ cup sugar	1 teaspoon pickling spice

1. Drain beets, reserving ⅓ cup of the beet liquid. Place beets in a 1-quart casserole with sugar, beet liquid, and vinegar. Tie pickling spice in a small square of cheesecloth and add to beets.
2. Cook, covered, on HIGH for 4 to 5 minutes, or until mixture comes to a boil.
3. Cool and remove bag of spices. Refrigerate up to 2 weeks.

Broccoli

4 servings

Peel stems off a bunch of broccoli that weighs about 1½ pounds. Remove leaves and cut off a slice from tough bottom. Split stems about 1 inch up to make for faster, more even cooking. Place in a 1½-quart casserole with the split stem ends arranged toward the sides of the dish. Add ¼ cup water. Cook, covered, on HIGH for 8 minutes. Let stand, covered, for 2 minutes.

Frozen Broccoli

2 to 3 servings

Place a 10-ounce package of frozen broccoli in a 1-quart casserole, icy side up. Cook, covered, for 7 to 9 minutes, or until tender. Rearrange broccoli halfway through cooking time.

Broccoli Indienne

3 to 4 servings

1 bunch broccoli, about 1½ pounds
⅓ cup chicken bouillon
1 bay leaf
¼ teaspoon thyme

2 tablespoons lemon juice·
1 tablespoon butter or margarine
Salt to taste

1. Wash broccoli. Cut off tough bottom stalks and discard. Remove leaves and peel tough skin from stalks. Cut stems in chunks, leaving flowerets intact.
2. Place stem chunks on sides and flowerets in center of a 1½-quart casserole. Add chicken bouillon, bay leaf, and thyme.
3. Cook, covered, on HIGH for 5 to 7 minutes, or just until tender.
4. Discard bay leaf and add lemon juice and butter. Toss lightly and season to taste with salt.

Frozen Brussels Sprouts

3 to 4 servings

Place a 10-ounce package frozen brussels sprouts in a 1-quart casserole. Add ¼ cup water. Cook, covered, on HIGH for 9 to 11 minutes, or until tender, stirring once during cooking period.

Cabbage

3 to 4 servings

Select a fresh-leafed head that is heavy for its size. New cabbage should be very green in color, though rather loose-leafed. Mature heads are paler in color and very solid. Red cabbage makes a pleasant change and is selected and cooked the same way as green cabbage.

Remove outer leaves of cabbage and wash whole head under running water. Cut in quarters. Remove most of core.

With a sharp knife, thinly slice ½ medium head of cabbage into medium-size shreds. Place in a 1½-quart casserole with 2 tablespoons water. Cook, covered, on HIGH for 6 minutes, stirring once during cooking time. Cover and let stand 2 minutes. Season to taste.

Norwegian Cabbage

3 to 4 servings

½ head cabbage
½ cup dairy sour cream

½ teaspoon caraway seeds
Salt and pepper to taste

1. Shred cabbage. Cook on HIGH for 6 to 7 minutes, or until tender. Drain.
2. Toss lightly with sour cream and caraway seeds. Season to taste with salt and pepper. Serve hot.

OPPOSITE: *Baked Potatoes, page 107; Cauliflower and Tomatoes, page 105.*

Sweet and Sour Cabbage

4 to 6 servings

4 cups shredded cabbage
2 apples, peeled, cored, and finely chopped
¼ cup brown sugar

1 teaspoon salt
⅛ teaspoon pepper
½ cup butter
¼ cup vinegar

1. Place cabbage in a 1½-quart casserole. Combine remaining ingredients. Pour over cabbage.
2. Cook, covered, on HIGH for 6 to 7 minutes, or until cabbage is tender. Stir once during cooking period.

Stuffed Eggplant

4 servings

2 medium eggplants
2 medium onions, chopped
1 pound ground lamb
1 beef bouillon cube
1 can (8 ounces) tomato sauce

½ teaspoon oregano
2 tablespoons chopped parsley
½ teaspoon salt
¼ teaspoon pepper
½ cup dry bread crumbs

1. Wash eggplant and cut in half lengthwise. Scoop out insides, leaving a shell 1 inch thick. Chop eggplant pulp in medium chunks. Set aside.
2. Put onion in a 1½-quart casserole. Crumble in lamb. Cook, covered, on HIGH for about 5 minutes, or just until lamb loses pink color. Drain fat.
3. Dissolve bouillon cube in ½ cup hot water. Stir into cooked lamb with 3 tablespoons tomato sauce and the chopped eggplant pulp.
4. Cook, covered, on HIGH for about 5 minutes, stirring occasionally.
5. Remove from oven; stir in oregano, parsley, salt, and pepper. Fill eggplant halves with mixture. Sprinkle bread crumbs over top. Streak remaining tomato sauce over top of crumbs.
6. Place eggplant halves in a glass baking dish. Cook, covered, on REHEAT for 8 minutes, or just until eggplant is tender.

Stuffed Green Peppers

4 to 6 servings

4 large green peppers
1 pound ground beef
1 medium onion, finely chopped
1 teaspoon salt

¼ teaspoon pepper
1½ cups cooked rice
1 can (16 ounces) tomato sauce

1. Wash peppers. Cut in half lengthwise and remove seeds and white membrane.
2. Crumble beef into a 1½-quart casserole. Add onion. Cook, uncovered, on HIGH for about 5 minutes, stirring once during cooking period. Cook until meat loses its red color.
3. Stir in salt, pepper, rice, and half of the tomato sauce. Fill green pepper halves with mixture, mounding mixture on top. Place in a glass baking dish. Top each pepper with a dribble of remaining tomato sauce.
4. Cook, covered, on HIGH for 8 to 10 minutes, or just until peppers are tender.

Cooked Rice
4 to 6 servings

2½ cups water
1 tablespoon butter or margarine

1 teaspoon salt
1 cup long-grained rice

1. Put water in a 2-quart casserole. Cook, uncovered, on HIGH just until water is boiling.
2. Add butter, salt, and rice and stir. Cook, covered, on HIGH for 10 minutes.
3. Remove. Cover and let stand for 10 minutes.
4. Stir with a fork to fluff before serving.

Eggs in Nests
8 servings

8 small, firm-ripe tomatoes
¼ cup chopped parsley
¼ cup butter or margarine

1 large onion, chopped
8 eggs
Salt and pepper to taste

1. Cut tops from tomatoes. Scoop out pulp and turn shells upside down on paper towels to drain. Discard seeds, chop pulp, and mix with parsley.
2. Combine butter and onion in a small mixing bowl. Cook, covered, on HIGH for about 4 minutes. Add parsley-tomato pulp mixture.
3. Stir mixture well and divide into tomato shells. Break 1 egg into each tomato shell. Season lightly with salt and pepper.
4. Place tomatoes in a baking dish. Cook, covered, on BAKE for 1 to 1½ minutes, or until eggs are set to desired degree of doneness.

Carrots
3 to 4 servings

Wash carrots well. Very tiny fresh spring carrots may be left whole. Mature carrots should be scraped or peeled. Cut carrots into thin rounds or slivers. Prepare 6 medium carrots. Place in a 1- or 1½-quart casserole. Add 2 tablespoons water. Cook, covered, on HIGH for 6 to 7 minutes, stirring once during cooking period. Let stand, covered, for 1 minute.

Frozen Carrots
3 to 4 servings

Place a 10-ounce package frozen carrots in a 1-quart casserole, icy side up. Cook, covered, on HIGH for 7 to 8 minutes, stirring once during cooking time.

Cranberry Carrots
4 servings

6 to 8 carrots
¼ cup butter or margarine

¼ cup jellied cranberry sauce
Salt and pepper to taste

1. Cook carrots according to directions. Add about 1 minute to cooking time for the larger number of carrots.
2. Place butter in a 1½- to 2-quart casserole. Cook, covered, on HIGH for 1½ minutes, or until butter is melted.
3. Add cranberry sauce. Cook, covered, on HIGH for 1 minute. Stir and cook until cranberry sauce is melted.
4. Add cooked carrots and toss gently. Season to taste with salt and pepper.

Tangy Glazed Carrots

3 to 4 servings

6 carrots
⅓ cup orange juice
2 tablespoons sugar
¼ teaspoon ground cloves

¼ teaspoon salt
½ jar (5 ounces) pineapple cheese
   spread

1. Peel carrots. Slice into rounds. Cook according to directions.
2. Combine juice, sugar, cloves, salt, and cheese spread. Blend thoroughly. Pour mixture over hot cooked carrots.
3. Cook, uncovered, on HIGH for about 1½ minutes, or until cheese melts and mixture is piping hot.

Cauliflower

3 to 4 servings

Remove outer leaves and stalks from 1 medium head of cauliflower. Separate into flowerets. Place in a 1½-quart casserole. Add 2 to 3 tablespoons water. Cook, covered, on HIGH for 7 to 8 minutes, or until cauliflower is tender. Stir once during cooking period.

Frozen Cauliflower

3 to 4 servings

Place a 10-ounce package frozen cauliflower in a 1-quart casserole, icy side up. Add 2 tablespoons water. Cook, covered, on HIGH for 7 to 8 minutes, stirring once during cooking period.

Cheesed Cauliflower

4 servings

1 medium head cauliflower
3 tablespoons olive oil
1 large onion, thinly sliced
¼ teaspoon salt

Dash of pepper
¼ cup fine dry bread crumbs
¼ cup grated Cheddar cheese

1. Remove outer leaves and stalks from cauliflower. Separate into flowerets. Cook according to preceding directions.
2. Put olive oil in a 1-quart measure. Add onion. Cook, uncovered, on SAUTE for about 4 minutes, or until onions are limp. Stir once during cooking time.
3. Add salt, pepper, and bread crumbs.
4. Drain cauliflower and leave in original casserole. Top with hot onion mixture. Sprinkle cheese over top.
5. Cook, uncovered, on ROAST for 1½ to 2 minutes, or until cheese is melted and cauliflower is piping hot.

Cauliflower and Tomatoes

4 servings

1 medium head cauliflower
1 clove garlic
3 tablespoons olive oil

½ teaspoon salt
½ cup cooked tomatoes
2 tablespoons grated Parmesan cheese

1. Remove outer leaves and stalks from cauliflower. Separate into flowerets. Cook according to directions but undercook just slightly.
2. Combine garlic and olive oil in a 1½-quart casserole. Cook, uncovered, on HIGH for 1 minute.
3. Remove garlic. Add hot drained cauliflower to oil.
4. Cook, uncovered, on HIGH for 2 minutes.
5. Add salt and tomatoes. Cook, covered, on HIGH for 4 minutes, or until piping hot. Stir once during cooking time.
6. Sprinkle top with cheese and serve immediately.

Celery

3 servings

Remove leaves and trim roots from a bunch of celery. Separate into stalks and wash thoroughly. Scrape off any discoloration with a knife. Use outer branches for cooking. Reserve inner branches to serve raw.

Slice stalks crosswise into half-moons, about 1½ inches thick. Use 6 stalks, making about 4 cups slices. Place in a 1½-quart casserole. Add 3 to 4 tablespoons water. Cook, covered, on HIGH for 8 to 9 minutes, or just until crisply tender. Stir once during cooking period. Drain.

Sweet and Sour Celery

3 to 4 servings

2 cups thinly sliced celery
1 bay leaf
3 whole cloves
2 tablespoons sugar

3 tablespoons vinegar
2 tablespoons butter or margarine
Salt and pepper to taste

1. Place celery, bay leaf, cloves, and ¼ cup water in a 1½-quart casserole.
2. Cook, covered, on HIGH for 8 to 9 minutes, or just until celery is crisply tender.
3. Add sugar, vinegar, and butter. Toss lightly. Cook, covered, on HIGH for 1 minute, or until butter is melted and celery is hot. Season to taste.

Corn on the Cob

Just before cooking, remove husks, all silk, and any blemishes. Wrap each ear of corn in a piece of waxed paper and twist ends tightly together. Place in oven, with about 1 inch space in between. Cook no more than 4 ears of fresh corn at one time. Cook on HIGH for 6 to 7 minutes, or until tender.

Another method for fresh corn on the cob is to strip the corn and place in a baking dish. Cook 4 ears of corn in an 8-inch square baking dish, covered, on HIGH for 8 minutes. Let stand 2 minutes before serving.

Frozen Cut Corn

3 to 4 servings

Place a 10-ounce package frozen kernel corn in a 1-quart casserole. Cook, covered, on HIGH for 5 to 6 minutes, stirring once during cooking period.

Note: Good with ham or pork chops for a hearty winter dinner.

Corn Pudding

4 servings

2 tablespoons butter or margarine	2 cups milk
2 tablespoons all-purpose flour	2 eggs, well beaten
1 can (1 pound) whole kernel corn, drained	1 teaspoon salt
	½ teaspoon pepper

1. Melt butter in a 1½-quart casserole on ROAST for 30 seconds.
2. Stir in flour to make a smooth paste. Add remaining ingredients and blend well.
3. Cook, covered, on HIGH for 9 minutes. Stir once during cooking period.
4. Cook, covered, on WARM for 3 minutes before serving.

Note: Good with ham or pork chops for a hearty winter dinner.

Saucy Eggplant

6 servings

4 slices bacon	2 teaspoons salt
1 medium onion, chopped	¼ teaspoon pepper
1 medium green pepper, seeded and chopped	1 can (8 ounces) tomato sauce
1 1-pound eggplant	½ cup grated Parmesan cheese

1. Place bacon on inverted saucer in an oblong glass baking dish. Cover with waxed paper. Cook on HIGH for about 5 minutes, or until bacon is crisp. Reserve bacon and drippings.
2. Put onion and pepper in a 1½-quart casserole. Pour bacon fat over top of onion.
3. Cook, covered, on HIGH for 4 minutes.
4. Peel eggplant and cut in cubes. Add to onion mixture in casserole with salt, pepper, tomato sauce, and 1 cup water.
5. Cook, covered, on HIGH for 6 minutes.
6. Remove from oven and sprinkle cheese over top of mixture. Crumble bacon and sprinkle over top of cheese.
7. Cook, covered, on HIGH for 6 minutes.
8. Cook, covered, on WARM for 4 minutes before serving.

Sautéed Mushrooms

2 to 4 servings

½ pound fresh mushrooms	⅓ cup butter or margarine
1 clove garlic, minced	

1. Clean mushrooms and slice. Put in an 8-inch round dish or a skillet. Add garlic and butter.

2. Cook, covered, on SAUTE for 4 to 5 minutes.
3. Serve with roast beef or steak, or on crisp toast as a main dish.

Peas   4 servings

Shell 2 pounds fresh peas and place in a 1½-quart casserole. Add 2 to 3 tablespoons water. Cook, covered, on HIGH for 7 to 8 minutes, stirring once during cooking time. Season to taste and serve.

Frozen Peas   3 to 4 servings

Place a 10-ounce package frozen peas in a 1-quart casserole, icy side up. Cook, covered, on HIGH for 5 to 6 minutes, stirring once during cooking time.

Baked Potatoes

Select baking potatoes of uniform size if possible so that they will all be cooked at the same time. Scrub potatoes with a stiff brush. Remove any bad spots with a sharp knife. Cut a thin slice from one end of each potato. Prick entire surface of potato with the tines of a fork.

Place potatoes on paper towels in the oven at least 1 inch apart. Cook given amount of time. It is easy to test potatoes with a fork or skewer to determine when they are done, so try shorter cooking time first and then increase as needed. To hold potatoes, wrap in aluminum foil.

1 medium potato, on HIGH for 4½ to 6 minutes
2 medium potatoes, on HIGH for 7 to 9 minutes
4 medium potatoes, on HIGH for 11 to 13 minutes

Boiled Potatoes   4 servings

Potatoes should be cut in quarters if they are small, in eighths if they are larger. The pieces should all be about the same size for uniform cooking. Peel 4 medium potatoes and cut up. Place in a 1½-quart casserole. Cover with water. Cook, covered, on HIGH for 12 to 16 minutes, or until potatoes are tender.

Hashed Potatoes   4 servings

⅓ cup butter or margarine   4 baked potatoes, cold
½ cup coarsely chopped onions   Salt and pepper to taste

1. Put butter and onion in a 1½-quart casserole. Cook, uncovered, on ROAST for 4 to 5 minutes, stirring occasionally.
2. Peel potatoes and cut in small chunks. Stir into onion in casserole. Season to taste. Cook, uncovered, on HIGH for 4 to 5 minutes, stirring occasionally.

Scalloped Potatoes

6 to 8 servings

5 cups (about 6 medium) peeled and thinly sliced raw potatoes
3 onions, sliced
Salt and pepper to taste
3 teaspoons dry mustard, divided
3 tablespoons grated Parmesan cheese, divided

3 tablespoons all-purpose flour, divided
3 tablespoons butter or margarine
3 cups milk
Paprika

1. Line bottom of a 3-quart casserole with one-third of the potatoes and cover with one-third of the onion. Add salt and pepper to taste, sprinkle on 1 teaspoon mustard, 1 tablespoon cheese, and 1 tablespoon flour. Repeat process twice with remaining potatoes, onion, seasonings, cheese, and flour. Dot with butter. Pour milk over top. Sprinkle with paprika.
2. Cook, covered, on HIGH for 20 minutes.
3. Cook, uncovered, on ROAST for 15 minutes, or until potatoes are tender. Let stand for 5 minutes before serving.

Sweet Potatoes

4 servings

Select sweet potatoes of approximately the same size for uniform cooking. Scrub 4 medium-size sweet potatoes. Remove any spots or blemishes with a sharp knife. Prick entire surface of each potato with a fork. Place on paper towels at least 1 inch apart in the oven. Cook on HIGH for 8 to 11 minutes, or until tender.

Candied Sweet Potatoes

6 servings

6 medium sweet potatoes
1 cup brown sugar, firmly packed

2 tablespoons butter or margarine

1. Cook sweet potatoes according to preceding directions. Peel and slice. Arrange in a 2-quart casserole.
2. Combine sugar, butter, and 1/3 cup water in a 1-quart measure. Cook, uncovered, on ROAST for 3 to 4 minutes, or until mixture is well blended and hot.
3. Pour over top of potatoes. Cook, covered, on HIGH for 7 to 8 minutes, or until heated through, spooning glaze over potatoes occasionally.

White Sauce

1 cup

2 tablespoons butter or margarine
2 tablespoons flour
½ teaspoon salt

Dash of pepper
1 cup milk

1. In a 1-quart measure, melt butter on ROAST for 30 seconds.
2. Stir in flour, salt, and pepper. Cook, uncovered, on HIGH for 30 seconds.
3. Gradually stir in milk. Cook, uncovered, on HIGH for 3 to 4 minutes, stirring during last half of cooking time. Remove and stir briskly.

Variations: For a thick white sauce use 3 tablespoons butter and 3 tablespoons flour with 1 cup milk. For a thin white sauce use 1 tablespoon butter and 1 tablespoon flour.

Sandwiches

Hot dogs are a kid's best friend. In the microwave oven they cook so fast that even the kids can't complain about starving while waiting for lunch to be ready. The franks can be cooked alone or popped into a bun, and the whole thing done in no time. Open-faced or closed, meat or fish, to be eaten from a plate or in the hand—delicious sandwiches of all kinds are prepared as if by magic in the microwave oven.

Brapples

4 servings

2 to 3 medium apples
¼ teaspoon lemon juice
¾ cup brown sugar

½ cup chopped walnuts
4 slices white bread, buttered
4 slices process American cheese

1. Peel, core, and slice apples in very thin slices.
2. Mix with lemon juice, brown sugar, and walnuts.
3. Divide over bread slices. Top with cheese.
4. Place in a 9-inch square dish.
5. Cook, uncovered, on HIGH for 2 to 3 minutes, or until apples are tender.

Variation: Turn these into a last-minute dessert by topping each with a table-spoon of sour cream and a sprinkling of brown sugar and nuts.

Bermuda Grill

6 servings

2 cups chopped Bermuda onions
1 teaspoon salt
¼ teaspoon white pepper

½ cup Sauterne
12 slices Swiss cheese
12 slices rye bread, toasted

1. Place chopped onion in a shallow dish; sprinkle with salt and pepper. Add Sauterne.
2. Cover and let stand at least 1 hour, stirring every 15 minutes; drain.
3. Place a slice of cheese on each of 6 toast slices.
4. Divide marinated onion over sandwiches and top with another slice of cheese, then a second slice of bread.
5. Place each sandwich on a paper plate. Cook one at a time on REHEAT for 1 minute, or until cheese is melted.

Hot Salad Cheesewiches

4 servings

1 cup shredded Cheddar cheese
½ cup diced cucumber
1 tablespoon minced onion
¼ cup dairy sour cream
⅛ teaspoon pepper

⅛ teaspoon chili powder
4 slices bread
4 large thick tomato slices
8 slices dill pickle
Paprika

1. Combine cheese, cucumber, onion, sour cream, and seasonings.
2. Toast bread lightly. Place each slice of bread on a paper plate.
3. Arrange a tomato slice and 2 pickle slices on each slice of bread.
4. Divide the cheese mixture over the 4 slices, and sprinkle with paprika.
5. Cook each sandwich separately on REHEAT for 1 to 1½ minutes, or until cheese melts and mixture is thoroughly heated.

Baked Brunchwiches

6 servings

12 to 14 slices white bread	6 eggs
Butter or margarine	2 cups milk
½ pound grated Cheddar cheese	½ teaspoon salt
1 teaspoon dry mustard	Paprika

1. Remove crust from bread slices. Butter each slice and cut in quarters or small chunks. Put a layer of bread in a 2- to 3-quart casserole. Sprinkle half the cheese over bread. Sprinkle half the mustard over cheese. Repeat layers with bread, cheese, and mustard.
2. Beat eggs with milk and salt. Pour over top of bread and cheese layers. Sprinkle generously with paprika.
3. Cover with foil or casserole lid and refrigerate overnight.
4. Cook on BAKE for 15 minutes.
5. Cook on HIGH for 10 minutes.
6. Remove from oven and cover with foil. Let stand 3 to 4 minutes before serving.

Cheese Roll-Ups

6 servings

4 slices bacon	¼ teaspoon Worcestershire sauce
1 loaf (1 pound) unsliced white bread	1 can (10½ ounces) condensed cream
1 cup grated process American cheese	of mushroom soup, undiluted
¼ cup chopped stuffed olives	¼ cup milk

1. Cook bacon according to directions on page 60 and reserve.
2. Cut crusts from loaf and cut loaf into 6 horizontal slices.
3. Crumble bacon and combine with cheese, olives, Worcestershire, and ⅓ cup of the mushroom soup.
4. Spread 3 tablespoons of the mixture on each slice of bread. Roll up, jelly-roll fashion.
5. Place each roll-up on a paper plate. Cook one at a time on HIGH for 1½ minutes, or until heated through.
6. Combine remaining mushroom soup and milk in a 2-cup glass measuring cup. Cook on BAKE for 4 to 4½ minutes, or until piping hot.
7. Serve mushroom sauce over roll-ups.

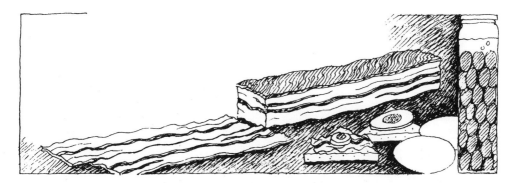

FOLLOWING PAGES: Left, *Reuben Sandwich, page 115;* right, *Hot Dogs and Sausage and Pepper Hero, page 116.*

Ranchburgers

6 servings

6 slices bacon
1½ cups grated process American
   cheese
2 tablespoons finely chopped onion

¼ cup catsup
1 tablespoon prepared mustard
6 sandwich buns, split

1. Cook bacon according to directions on page 60. Crumble bacon and combine with remaining ingredients except buns.
2. Spread 3 tablespoons cheese mixture on bottom half of each bun and cover with bun top.
3. Wrap each sandwich in waxed paper and twist ends of paper.
4. Cook each sandwich separately on REHEAT for 1 to 1½ minutes, or until heated through.

Second-Act Ham

3 to 4 servings

¾ cup hollandaise sauce
4 slices bread, toasted
Ham slices from leftover baked ham

1 can (8 ounces) asparagus, drained,
   or 9 to 12 fresh asparagus, cooked
2 hard-cooked eggs, sliced (optional)

1. Prepare hollandaise sauce, using your favorite recipe. Cover with waxed paper and set aside.
2. Arrange toast, cut in quarters, in individual casseroles. Put desired amount of ham on top of toast. Arrange 3 or 4 asparagus spears on top of ham. Add ½ egg, sliced, on top if desired.
3. Cook, covered, 1 casserole at a time, on BAKE for about 2 minutes, or until heated through.
4. Top with hollandaise sauce. Cover with waxed paper and heat on BAKE for 1 minute. If hollandaise sauce is cold, double the heating time.

Sardine Buns

6 servings

¼ pound process American cheese,
   cubed
5 hard-cooked eggs, chopped
½ cup drained mashed sardines
1 tablespoon minced green pepper

2 tablespoons minced onion
3 tablespoons chopped stuffed olives
2 tablespoons pickle relish, drained
½ cup mayonnaise
6 hamburger buns, split and buttered

1. Combine all ingredients except buns.
2. Fill each bun with cheese mixture.
3. Wrap each sandwich in waxed paper and twist ends of paper.
4. Cook, one at a time, on REHEAT for 1 to 1½ minutes, or until rolls are hot.

Note: These may be prepared in advance and refrigerated in their waxed paper wrapping. Cook before serving.

Hot Swiss Tuna

4 servings

4 hamburger buns
1 can (6½ or 7 ounces) tuna fish, drained and flaked
½ cup finely shredded Swiss cheese
1 cup chopped celery

¼ cup mayonnaise
2 tablespoons catsup
1 teaspoon lemon juice
Salt and pepper to taste

1. Split hamburger buns.
2. Combine tuna, cheese, celery, mayonnaise, catsup, and lemon juice. Season to taste with salt and pepper.
3. Divide tuna mixture among four buns.
4. Wrap each sandwich in waxed paper and twist ends of paper.
5. Cook one at a time on REHEAT for 1 to 1½ minutes, or until rolls are hot.

Barbecued Beef Strips on Buns

6 servings

½ cup butter or margarine
1 pound top round steak, cut into thin strips
1 teaspoon salt
⅛ teaspoon garlic salt
⅛ teaspoon pepper
1 can (10½ ounces) beef broth

1 can (8 ounces) tomato paste
2 tablespoons cornstarch
1 teaspoon sugar
1 can (4 ounces) sliced mushrooms, drained
¼ cup dry red wine
6 buns

1. Put butter in a 2- or 3-quart casserole. Cook, uncovered, on HIGH for 1 minute, or just until butter melts.
2. Put strips of meat in casserole and toss lightly so that meat is coated with butter. Add salt, garlic salt, and pepper.
3. Cook, uncovered, on HIGH for 5 to 6 minutes, stirring once.
4. Add beef broth and tomato paste. Combine cornstarch and sugar and stir into mixture.
5. Cook, covered, on HIGH for 4 minutes, stirring once.
6. Add mushrooms and wine. Cook, covered, on HIGH for 1 to 2 minutes, or until mushrooms are hot.
7. Let stand, covered, on LOW for 4 minutes before serving.
8. Serve beef strips, with sauce, in heated buns.

Reuben Sandwich

4 servings

8 slices dark rye or pumpernickel bread
Butter or margarine
½ pound thinly sliced corned beef

1 can (8 ounces) sauerkraut, drained
Thousand Island dressing
4 slices Swiss cheese

1. Toast bread. Butter lightly.
2. Arrange sliced corned beef on 4 slices of toast. Divide sauerkraut among sandwiches. Top with Thousand Island dressing. Top each with a slice of Swiss cheese. Top with other slices of toast, buttered side down.
3. Place each sandwich on a paper plate.
4. Cook one at a time on REHEAT for about 1 minute, or just until cheese is melted.

115

Sausage and Pepper Hero
4 servings

4 Italian sausages

½ cup prepared barbecue sauce

1 green pepper, seeded and cut in strips

4 hero rolls

1. Place a layer of paper towels in an 8-inch square dish. Place sausage on towels. Cover with paper towels.
2. Cook on HIGH for 8 minutes, turning halfway through cooking period. Drain off fat and reserve.
3. Cook barbecue sauce with pepper strips in a 2-cup measure on HIGH for 2 minutes.
4. Split hero rolls almost in half. Place 1 cooked sausage in each roll. Top with one-quarter of the sauce and peppers. Wrap each roll in waxed paper and twist ends of paper.
5. Cook, one at a time, on HIGH for 1 to 1½ minutes, or until rolls are piping hot.

Hot Dogs
1 serving

1 frankfurter roll

Prepared mustard

Pickle relish

1 frankfurter

1. Spread roll with mustard and relish. Place hot dog in roll. Wrap in waxed paper and twist ends securely.
2. Cook one hot dog on HIGH for 45 seconds. Cook 2 hot dogs at a time on HIGH for 1½ minutes; cook 3 hot dogs on HIGH for 2½ to 3 minutes; cook 4 hot dogs on HIGH for 3 to 3½ minutes, or until piping hot.

Beans and Things
6 servings

6 slices bacon, cut in pieces

1 medium onion, chopped

4 frankfurters, cut in small pieces

1 teaspoon prepared mustard

1 teaspoon catsup

1 can (1 pound) pork and beans in tomato sauce

6 slices toast

1. Put bacon pieces in 1½-quart casserole.
2. Cook, covered, on HIGH for 2 to 3 minutes. Stir.
3. Add chopped onion.
4. Cook, covered, on HIGH for 2 minutes. Stir well.
5. Add frankfurters. Cook, covered, on HIGH for about 3 minutes. Add mustard, catsup, and beans and mix well.
6. Cook, covered, on HIGH for about 4 minutes, or until hot, stirring once during cooking period. Serve over toast.

116

OPPOSITE: *Cheeseburger, page 120.*

Asparagus Egg Specials

6 servings

6 slices white bread
2 tablespoons soft butter or margarine
3 hard-cooked eggs, sliced
24 cooked green asparagus spears
(see page 94)

Salt and pepper to taste
1 can (8 ounces) tomato sauce
¼ teaspoon sugar
½ teaspoon oregano
2 tablespoons slivered almonds

1. Toast bread and spread lightly with butter.
2. Arrange egg slices on toast and top each toast slice with 4 asparagus spears. Sprinkle with salt and pepper.
3. Combine tomato sauce, sugar, and oregano.
4. Place toast slices in a 9-inch square dish. Pour tomato sauce over and sprinkle with nuts.
5. Cook on HIGH for 2 to 3 minutes, or until heated through.

Chicken Crumpets

8 servings

4 tablespoons butter or margarine
¼ cup all-purpose flour
1 teaspoon salt
⅛ teaspoon pepper
2 cups milk

3 tablespoons sherry
2 cups diced cooked chicken
Paprika
4 crumpets or English muffins
8 baked ham slices

1. Place butter in a 1-quart measure. Cook on ROAST for 30 seconds, or until butter is melted.
2. Stir in flour, salt, and pepper. Cook on HIGH for 30 seconds.
3. Stir in milk. Cook on HIGH for 3 to 4 minutes, stirring twice during cooking time.
4. Remove from oven and stir in sherry, chicken, and a dash of paprika.
5. Split, toast, and butter crumpets or English muffins. Place each on a paper plate.
6. Place 1 slice of ham on each crumpet half. Divide chicken mixture over ham slices and sprinkle lightly with paprika.
7. Cook 4 at a time on HIGH for about 2 minutes, or until heated through.

Chicken Tacos

10 to 12 servings

½ cup chopped onions
2 tablespoons butter or margarine
2 cups coarsely diced cooked chicken
1 can (7½ ounces) taco sauce
¼ teaspoon salt

¼ teaspoon garlic salt
10 to 12 fully cooked taco shells
Grated Cheddar cheese
Shredded lettuce
Chopped fresh tomatoes

1. Cook onion and butter in a 1-quart measure on SAUTE for about 3 minutes.
2. Add chicken, taco sauce, salt, and garlic salt. Cover with a paper towel.

3. Cook on HIGH for about 5 minutes, or until mixture thickens and is hot.
4. Spoon hot filling into taco shells. Serve immediately with side dishes filled with cheese, lettuce, and tomato to sprinkle over hot filling.

Turkey Glory   6 servings

6 slices cooked turkey
6 slices white bread, toasted and
   buttered
1 package (8 ounces) cream cheese,
   at room temperature

1 cup milk
1/2 cup grated Parmesan cheese
1/4 teaspoon garlic salt
1/2 cup sliced stuffed olives
Paprika

1. Place turkey on toast.
2. Put softened cream cheese in a 1-quart measure. Gradually add milk to cheese, mixing until well blended.
3. Cook on BAKE for 3 minutes.
4. Stir. Cook on BAKE for 2 minutes.
5. Remove from oven and stir in Parmesan cheese, garlic salt, and olives.
6. Cover each sandwich with sauce; sprinkle with paprika.

Sloppy Joe Sandwich   6 servings

1 pound ground beef
½ cup chopped onions
½ cup chopped green pepper
½ teaspoon paprika
1 can (8 ounces) tomato sauce

1 teaspoon salt
Pinch of sugar
Freshly ground pepper to taste
Toasted hamburger buns

1. Crumble beef in a 2-quart casserole. Add onion, pepper, and paprika.
2. Cook, uncovered, on HIGH for 4 minutes, or until meat loses its red color. Stir once during cooking time.
3. Break up meat with a fork. Add remaining ingredients except buns and blend well.
4. Cook, covered, on HIGH for 10 minutes, stirring occasionally.
5. Spoon onto bottom half of toasted hamburger buns; cover with top half.

Note: The Sloppy Joe mixture can be made up well in advance and kept in the refrigerator. To serve, remove any congealed fat on top of mixture. Spoon desired amount of meat on hamburger buns or hard rolls, spreading mixture out to edges. Place single serving on a small plate. Heat for 1 to 1½ minutes, until mixture is piping hot.

Witches' Brew Heroes

6 servings

1 medium onion, chopped	½ teaspoon chili powder
1 small green pepper, seeded and chopped	¼ teaspoon salt
	¼ teaspoon sugar
1 clove garlic, peeled and halved	¼ teaspoon hot-pepper sauce
1 pound ground beef, crumbled	⅛ teaspoon ground cumin
1 can (1 pound) whole tomatoes	6 hero rolls

1. Combine onion, green pepper, garlic, and beef in a 2-quart casserole.
2. Cook, uncovered, on HIGH for 4 minutes, or until meat loses its red color. Stir once to break up meat.
3. Break up large meat chunks with a fork. Mash tomatoes with a fork so that tomatoes are in small chunks. Add to meat mixture with chili powder, salt, sugar, hot-pepper sauce, and cumin.
4. Cook, covered, on HIGH for 10 minutes, stirring once.
5. Remove garlic. Serve on hero rolls.

Paul Bunyans

6 servings

1 pound ground beef	Freshly ground pepper to taste
½ cup finely chopped onion	½ teaspoon poultry seasoning
½ cup finely chopped green pepper	½ teaspoon hot-pepper sauce
½ cup chopped pitted ripe olives	½ teaspoon chili powder
1 can (6 ounces) tomato paste	1 teaspoon Worcestershire sauce
1 teaspoon salt	Toasted hamburger buns

1. Crumble beef into a 2-quart casserole. Add onion and green pepper.
2. Cook, uncovered, on HIGH for 4 minutes, or until meat has lost its red color. Stir once during cooking time.
3. Break up meat chunks with a fork. Add olives, tomato paste, salt, pepper, poultry seasoning, hot-pepper sauce, chili powder, and Worcestershire. Stir well. Add 1 to 2 tablespoons of water if mixture is dry.
4. Cook, covered, on HIGH for 10 minutes, stirring once.
5. Serve immediately on toasted buns.

Cheeseburgers

4 servings

1 pound ground beef	4 hamburger buns, toasted
Salt and pepper	4 slices process American cheese

1. Season ground beef to taste with salt and pepper. Shape into 4 patties. Place in an 8-inch square baking dish.
2. Cook, covered with waxed paper, on REHEAT for 2 minutes.
3. Turn patties over. Cook, covered, on REHEAT for 2 minutes, or to the desired degree of doneness.
4. Place 1 patty on each hamburger bun. Top with a slice of cheese. Place each bun on a small paper plate.
5. Cook 1 or 2 at a time on REHEAT for 1 minute, or until cheese melts.

Open-Face Hamburgers

6 servings

1 pound ground beef
1 teaspoon salt
1 teaspoon oregano
½ teaspoon dry mustard
Freshly ground pepper to taste
1 tablespoon instant minced onion

½ cup tomato juice
1 cup shredded Cheddar cheese
3 hamburger buns, halved and toasted
6 slices tomato
2 tablespoons butter or margarine

1. Crumble ground beef into a 1½-quart casserole or an 8-inch round glass cake dish.
2. Cook, uncovered, on HIGH for 5 to 6 minutes, or until meat has lost its red color. Stir once during cooking time.
3. Break up meat with a fork. Add salt, oregano, dry mustard, pepper, onion, tomato juice, and cheese. Stir thoroughly.
4. Cook, covered, on BAKE for 2 to 3 minutes, or until cheese is melted and mixture is piping hot.
5. Place toasted hamburger halves on a broiler pan. Spoon hamburger mixture on top of each bun. Top each with a slice of tomato. Dot with butter. Place under broiler on conventional range and broil until tomatoes are lightly browned.

Old Mystic

6 servings

1 can (7½ ounces) crab meat, drained
1 can (5 ounces) shrimp, drained
2 packages (3 ounces each) cream cheese, at room temperature
½ cup chopped almonds
2 tablespoons dry white wine
2 teaspoons lemon juice
1 teaspoon minced onion

1 teaspoon prepared horseradish
1 teaspoon prepared mustard
½ teaspoon salt
¼ teaspoon white pepper
⅛ teaspoon cayenne
6 French rolls
⅓ cup shredded Gruyere cheese

1. Pick over crab meat and remove any bits of shells or cartilage. Combine with shrimp and cream cheese and blend well. Add almonds, white wine, lemon juice, onion, horseradish, mustard, salt, pepper, and cayenne.
2. Remove top third from each roll and scoop out inside, being careful not to puncture shell. Spoon mixture evenly into 6 shells. Sprinkle cheese over top of filling. Place tops on rolls.
3. Place 2 rolls at a time on paper towels or paper plates in oven. Cook on HIGH for 1 to 1½ minutes, or until filling is piping hot and cheese has melted.

Turkey Gobble-Up

6 servings

6 English muffins
Butter
6 slices bacon
1 large avocado
¼ cup mayonnaise
¼ cup dairy sour cream
1 tablespoon lemon juice

Dash of hot-pepper sauce
12 slices (1 ounce each) cooked turkey
   breast
12 slices tomato
1 jar (8 ounces) pasteurized process
   cheese spread

1. Split, toast, and butter English muffins.
2. Cut bacon strips into 4 pieces each. Place on a paper towel in an oblong baking dish. Cover with a paper towel. Cook on HIGH for 2 to 3 minutes.
3. Peel, seed, and mash avocado. Combine with mayonnaise, sour cream, lemon juice, and hot-pepper sauce.
4. Spread avocado mixture generously on each muffin half. Arrange 1 slice each turkey and tomato on each muffin half. Spread 1 tablespoon cheese on each tomato. Top each with 2 pieces of cooked bacon.
5. Place 6 halves in an oblong baking dish. Cook on ROAST for 1½ to 2 minutes, or until cheese is hot and bubbly.

Ham and Asparagus Cheese Sandwiches

4 servings

4 slices bread, toasted
4 slices thinly sliced ham

8 slices Swiss cheese
1 can (15 ounces) asparagus spears

1. Place toasted bread in a baking dish.
2. Cover each slice with 1 slice ham, 1 slice cheese, and 5 asparagus spears.
3. Cook on HIGH for 3 to 4 minutes, or until cheese is piping hot.
4. Garnish with paprika if desired.

Beverages

Single servings of coffee or cocoa, made in mugs or paper cups, are heated in seconds and are certainly a boon for the busy homemaker. If beverages cool off, the microwave oven will bring them back to serving temperature in a flash. Don't forget that milk boils over easily and rapidly —so when making beverages with milk, do not fill the container, large or small, to the brim.

Mulled Wine

8 to 10 servings

1 cup sugar

2 pieces (1 inch each) stick cinnamon

1 lemon, sliced

24 whole cloves

4 cups orange juice

1 quart Burgundy wine

1. Combine sugar, cinnamon, lemon, and cloves with ½ cup water in a 3-quart casserole.
2. Heat on HIGH for 2 minutes.
3. Add orange juice and Burgundy.
4. Heat on HIGH for 7 to 8 minutes.
5. Garnish with lemon or pineapple slices, if desired.

Hot Toddy

1 serving

1 teaspoon sugar

1 piece (1 inch) stick cinnamon

1 slice lemon, studded with 2 cloves

2 ounces bourbon

1. Combine sugar, cinnamon, and lemon slice with ½ cup water in a 1-cup measuring cup.
2. Cook on HIGH for 2½ minutes.
3. Meantime, place bourbon in a serving cup or mug.
4. Remove hot mixture from oven and pour over bourbon. Stir and serve.

Mulled Pineapple Juice

10 servings

1 can (46 ounces) pineapple juice

1 piece (2 inches) stick cinnamon

⅛ teaspoon ground nutmeg

⅛ teaspoon ground allspice

Dash ground cloves

1. Combine all ingredients in a 2-quart casserole.
2. Heat on HIGH for 7 to 8 minutes.

Spicy Apple Nog

5 to 6 servings

2 eggs, separated

¼ cup sugar

½ teaspoon salt

½ teaspoon ground cinnamon

Dash of ground nutmeg

⅔ cup apple juice

3 cups milk

½ cup heavy cream, whipped

1. Place egg yolks in a 2-quart casserole. Beat lightly with a fork.
2. Stir in sugar, salt, cinnamon, nutmeg, and apple juice until well blended. Stir in milk.
3. Cook on ROAST for 7 to 8 minutes, or until piping hot.
4. Meantime, beat egg whites in a 2-quart mixing bowl.
5. Remove milk mixture from oven and pour quickly over egg whites, stirring rapidly.
6. Top each serving with a mound of whipped cream.

124

OPPOSITE: *Hot Instant Tea, page 128; Instant Coffee, page 127; Instant Cocoa, Mulled Cider, Hot Spiced Cranberry Punch, page 126.*

Hot Spiced Cranberry Punch

6 servings

1½ cups cranberry juice cocktail
4 whole cloves
1 piece (2 inches) stick cinnamon
3 tablespoons sugar

1 can (6 ounces) frozen lemonade concentrate, thawed
3 orange slices, cut in half
6 maraschino cherries

1. Combine cranberry juice, cloves, and cinnamon stick with 1½ cups water in 1-quart measuring cup.
2. Cook on HIGH for 4 minutes.
3. Cover and let stand 1 minute.
4. Remove spices.
5. Stir in sugar until dissolved.
6. Blend in lemonade.
7. Cook on HIGH for 3 minutes.
8. Serve hot, garnished with half an orange slice and a maraschino cherry on a toothpick.

Mulled Cider

4 servings

3 cups apple cider
3 tablespoons brown sugar
⅛ teaspoon salt
Dash of ground nutmeg

½ teaspoon whole allspice
½ teaspoon whole cloves
1 stick cinnamon
2 orange slices, cut in half

1. Place apple cider, brown sugar, salt, and nutmeg in 1-quart measuring cup.
2. Tie allspice, cloves, and cinnamon in cheesecloth and drop into cider.
3. Cook on HIGH for 4 to 5 minutes. Let stand 5 minutes.
4. Remove spice bag and serve hot, garnished with orange slices.

Mexican Chocolate

4 servings

½ cup semisweet chocolate bits
1 tablespoon instant coffee
½ teaspoon vanilla extract

¼ teaspoon ground cinnamon
2 cups milk

1. Place chocolate, coffee, and ½ cup water in a 4-cup measuring cup.
2. Heat on HIGH for 2 minutes.
3. Remove from oven and stir in remaining ingredients.
4. Heat on HIGH for 4 minutes.

Instant Cocoa

1 serving

¾ cup milk
2 teaspoons instant cocoa mix

Marshmallows

1. Combine milk and cocoa in a 2-cup measuring cup.
2. Cook on ROAST for 2 minutes.
3. Add marshmallows and serve.

Slemp
4 servings

1 piece (1 inch) stick cinnamon
2 whole cloves
½ teaspoon ground mace
½ teaspoon instant tea

4 cups milk
Peel of half a lemon, cut in strips
⅛ teaspoon salt
2 tablespoons sugar

1. Tie cinnamon, cloves, mace, and tea in cheesecloth.
2. Place milk in a 2-quart casserole.
3. Add the bag of spices, lemon peel, and salt to milk.
4. Cook on HIGH for 4 to 5 minutes, or until hot.
5. Remove from oven and stir in sugar.
6. Cook on HIGH for 30 seconds.

Spicy Orange Coffee
6 servings

1 tablespoon sugar
6 whole cloves
2 pieces (1½ inches each) stick cinnamon

Peel of small orange, in strips
1 tablespoon instant coffee

1. Combine all ingredients with 1½ cups water in a 2-cup measuring cup.
2. Heat on HIGH for 4 to 5 minutes, or until piping hot.
3. Strain into demitasse cups.

Café au Lait
4 servings

4 teaspoons instant coffee
2 cups milk

Sugar (optional)

1. Place coffee and 1 cup water in a 4-cup measuring cup.
2. Stir in milk.
3. Cook on HIGH for 4 to 5 minutes, or until piping hot.
4. Sweeten to taste, if desired.

Viennese After-Dinner Coffee
8 servings

6 teaspoons instant coffee

¼ cup heavy cream, whipped

1. Combine coffee and 3 cups water in a 4-cup measuring cup.
2. Cook on HIGH for 4 to 5 minutes, or until piping hot.
3. Serve in demitasse cups.
4. Top each serving with whipped cream.

Instant Coffee
4 servings

4 to 5 teaspoons instant coffee

1. Combine coffee and 3 cups water in a 1-quart measuring cup.
2. Cook on HIGH 4 to 5 minutes, or until hot. To develop a richer flavor, let stand for 2 minutes.

Coffee Cream Punch   8 servings

6 tablespoons instant coffee   **Ground nutmeg**
1½ pints vanilla ice cream

1. Combine coffee and 4 cups water in a 1½-quart casserole.
2. Cook on HIGH for 5 to 6 minutes, or until piping hot.
3. Meantime, place ice cream in a 3-quart bowl.
4. Pour hot coffee over the ice cream; stir until melted.
5. Ladle into cups and sprinkle each serving with nutmeg.

Café Calypso   6 servings

4 cups milk   **½ cup heavy cream, whipped**
⅓ cup instant coffee   **Ground nutmeg**
¼ cup brown sugar

1. Place ⅓ cup water in a 2-quart casserole.
2. Heat on HIGH for 1 minute.
3. Add milk, coffee, and sugar.
4. Cook on HIGH for 4 to 5 minutes.
5. Serve hot, topped with whipped cream and a dash of nutmeg.

Hot Tea   4 servings

4 tea bags

1. Place 3 cups water in a 4-cup measuring cup.
2. Heat on HIGH for 5 minutes.
3. Add tea bags. Remove when desired strength of tea is obtained.

Hot Instant Tea   4 servings

5 to 6 teaspoons instant tea

1. Mix tea with 3 cups water in a 4-cup measuring cup.
2. Heat on HIGH for 5 minutes.

Iced Tea   4 servings

6 tea bags, or 2½ to 3 tablespoons   **3 to 4 tablespoons sugar**
instant tea   **Ice cubes**

1. Place 3 cups water in a 4-cup measuring cup.
2. Heat on HIGH for 5 minutes.
3. Add tea.
4. When desired strength is obtained, take out tea bags and stir in sugar until dissolved.
5. Serve over ice in tall glasses.

Desserts

Your microwave oven will cook puddings, custards, fruits, and cakes superbly. Cake baking is much faster than conventionally, producing a cake with a different, but delectable, look and texture. Cakes should be rotated during cooking time so that they will rise evenly and produce a smooth top. Test with a toothpick; if it comes out clean, the cake is done. As it cools, the top, which looks somewhat damp, will dry out. You will be pleased with the moist texture and taste.

When baking double-crust fruit pies, cook in the microwave oven until the fruit is cooked—a great time-saver—then continue baking in the conventional oven until the crust is brown and crisp.

Applesauce Cake

12 servings

1 cup applesauce	1 teaspoon ground cinnamon
⅞ cup brown sugar, firmly packed	½ teaspoon ground cloves
½ cup melted butter or margarine	1 teaspoon ground ginger
1¾ cups sifted all-purpose flour	½ cup seedless raisins
1 teaspoon baking soda	½ cup chopped nuts
½ teaspoon salt	

1. In a small bowl combine applesauce, sugar, and butter. Set aside.
2. Sift flour, baking soda, salt, and spices into a large mixing bowl. Add the applesauce mixture and blend well. Stir in raisins and nuts. Pour batter into a lightly greased 12- by 8- by 2-inch baking dish.
3. Cook on BAKE for 9 minutes.
4. Cook on HIGH for 6 minutes, or until done. Cake is done when a toothpick inserted in center comes out clean.
5. Let cool before serving.

Devil's Food Cake

2 8-inch layers

2 cups sifted all-purpose flour	½ cup cocoa
1¼ teaspoons baking soda	1 teaspoon vanilla extract
¼ teaspoon salt	½ cup buttermilk
½ cup shortening	2 eggs, lightly beaten
2 cups sugar	

1. Grease the bottoms of two 8-inch round cake dishes. Line the bottoms with 2 layers of waxed paper.
2. Sift together flour, baking soda, and salt. Set aside.
3. Cream together shortening, sugar, cocoa, and vanilla until light and fluffy.
4. Measure 1 cup water in a 2-cup measuring cup. Cook for about 2½ minutes, or until water comes to a boil. Let stand.
5. Stir boiling water, buttermilk, and eggs into creamed mixture and beat well. Add sifted dry ingredients all at once and beat well.
6. Divide mixture between prepared cake dishes.
7. Cook, uncovered, one layer at a time on BAKE for 5 minutes.
8. Cook on HIGH for 4 minutes. Remove from oven and let stand until cake is cool.
9. Turn out of dishes and cool thoroughly. Frost as desired.

Gingerbread

6 to 8 servings

1 package (14 ounces) gingerbread mix

1. Prepare gingerbread mix according to package directions, decreasing liquid by 2 tablespoons. Pour batter into an 8-inch round cake dish.

2. Bake, uncovered, on BAKE for 8 minutes.
3. Bake on HIGH for 3 to 4 minutes, or until cake is done.
4. Remove from oven and let stand a few minutes before cutting.

Pumpkin Raisin-Nut Cake

12 servings

½ cup shortening
1 cup sugar
2 eggs, lightly beaten
1 cup solid-pack cooked pumpkin
2 cups sifted all-purpose flour
4 teaspoons baking powder
1 teaspoon baking soda

1 teaspoon salt
2½ teaspoons ground cinnamon
½ teaspoon ground nutmeg
¼ teaspoon ground ginger
1 cup seedless raisins
1 cup chopped nuts

1. Cream shortening and sugar together until light and fluffy. Beat in eggs and pumpkin; beat well.
2. Sift together flour, baking powder, baking soda, salt, and spices. Stir into pumpkin mixture and blend well. Stir in raisins and nuts. Pour batter into a lightly greased 12- by 8- by 2-inch baking dish.
3. Cook on SIMMER for 9 minutes.
4. Cook on HIGH for 6 minutes, or until a toothpick inserted in center of cake comes out clean.
5. Let cool before serving.

Sour Cream Coffee Cake

1 8-inch cake

¼ cup butter or margarine
½ cup sugar
2 eggs
½ teaspoon vanilla extract
1½ cups sifted all-purpose flour
½ teaspoon baking soda
½ teaspoon baking powder

½ cup dairy sour cream
⅓ cup brown sugar, firmly packed
2 tablespoons flour
½ cup chopped nuts
⅛ teaspoon ground cinnamon
⅛ teaspoon salt
2 tablespoons butter or margarine

1. Cream together ¼ cup butter and sugar until light and fluffy. Add eggs and vanilla and beat thoroughly. Sift together flour, soda, and baking powder. Add to creamed mixture alternately with sour cream, blending well after each addition.
2. Combine remaining ingredients and mix until crumbly.
3. Spread half of the batter in an 8-inch round cake dish. Sprinkle with half of topping mix. Spread on remaining batter and sprinkle with remaining topping.
4. Cook on BAKE for 4 minutes.
5. Cook on HIGH for 3 minutes. Serve coffee cake warm.

FOLLOWING PAGES: Left, Gingerbread, page 130; Quick Boston Cream Pie and Pineapple Upside-Down Cake, page 135; right, Devil's Food Cake, page 130.

Spice Cake
12 servings

2 eggs	½ teaspoon ground allspice
1 cup sugar	½ teaspoon salt
2 tablespoons molasses	2 teaspoons baking powder
2 cups sifted all-purpose flour	1 teaspoon baking soda
1 teaspoon ground cinnamon	1 cup buttermilk
1 teaspoon ground cloves	⅔ cup cooking oil

1. Beat eggs until thick and lemon-colored. Beat in sugar and molasses until well blended.
2. Sift together flour, spices, salt, baking powder, and baking soda. Add to egg mixture alternately with buttermilk, mixing well after each addition. Stir in oil.
3. Pour batter into a lightly greased 12- by 8- by 2-inch baking dish.
4. Cook on BAKE for 9 minutes.
5. Cook on HIGH for 6 minutes, or until a toothpick inserted in center of cake comes out clean.
6. Let cool before serving.

Packaged Cake Mix
2 8-inch layers

1 package (1 pound 2½ ounces) cake mix

1. Grease the bottom of an 8-inch round cake dish. Place two 8-inch circles of waxed paper on bottom of dish.
2. Prepare cake mix according to package directions.
3. Pour one-half of the batter into the prepared cake dish.
4. Cook, uncovered, on BAKE for 7 minutes. Finish on HIGH 3 to 4 minutes.
5. Let stand a few minutes to cool. Turn out of pan and remove waxed paper from bottom of cake.
6. Repeat process for remaining layer.

Pound Cake
2 loaves

1 package (16 ounces) pound cake

1. Line the bottom of two 8- by 4-inch loaf pans with 2 layers of waxed paper.
2. Prepare cake mix according to package directions. Divide batter between two pans.
3. Cook, uncovered, 1 cake at a time on BAKE for 6 minutes.
4. Let stand in cake pan 3 minutes. Turn out, peel off paper, and let cool before serving.

Pineapple Upside-Down Cake

6 servings

2 tablespoons butter or margarine
½ cup firmly packed dark brown sugar
1 can (8¼ ounces) sliced pineapple, well drained, juice reserved

6 to 10 maraschino cherries, well drained
1 package (9 ounces) yellow cake mix
Whipped cream

1. Put butter and brown sugar in an 8-inch round cake dish.
2. Cook, uncovered, on ROAST for 2 minutes, or until butter and sugar are blended.
3. Smooth mixture over bottom of pan. Arrange pineapple slices on brown sugar and dot with maraschino cherries.
4. Prepare package mix according to directions, using ⅓ cup of the pineapple juice for part of the liquid and reducing the total liquid by 1 tablespoon.
5. Pour batter carefully into pan without disturbing pineapple or sugar mixture.
6. Cook, uncovered, on BAKE for 7 minutes.
7. Cook on HIGH for 3 to 4 minutes. Remove from oven and let stand 3 minutes.
8. Invert pan on serving plate and remove pan, leaving syrup and fruit on top of cake.
9. Serve with whipped cream.

Quick Boston Cream Pie

1 8-inch pie

1 package Boston cream pie mix

1. Prepare pudding from package according to package directions. Set aside.
2. Grease the bottom of an 8-inch round cake dish. Place 2 circles of waxed paper on bottom of pan.
3. Prepare cake mix according to package directions.
4. Cook, uncovered, on BAKE for 5 minutes. Cook on HIGH for 2 minutes, or until a toothpick inserted in center of cake comes out clean.
5. Cool in pan about 3 minutes. Turn out of pan onto cake cooler and peel off waxed paper.
6. Assemble finished cake according to package directions.

Nut Bread Mix

1 loaf

1 package (17 ounces) nut bread mix

1. Line the bottom of a 9- by 5- by 3-inch loaf pan with 2 layers of waxed paper.
2. Prepare mix according to package directions.
3. Pour into pan.
4. Cook, uncovered, on BAKE for 10 minutes.
5. Cook on HIGH for 3 minutes, or until a toothpick inserted in center of loaf comes out clean.

FOLLOWING PAGES: Left, *Apple Pie;* right, *Cherry Cheese Pie;* page 139.

Corn Muffins

8 muffins

1 package (8½ ounces) corn bread or muffin mix

1. Place paper liners in 8 custard cups.
2. Prepare muffin mix according to package directions. Divide mixture among prepared cups, filling them not more than half full.
3. Bake 4 at a time, uncovered, on BAKE for 4 to 5 minutes, or until a toothpick inserted in center comes out clean.
4. Let stand a few minutes, then turn out of cups.

Cupcakes

8 cupcakes

1 package (8 ounces) yellow cake mix

1. Place paper liners in 8 custard cups.
2. Prepare cake mix according to package directions, reducing liquid by 1 tablespoon. Pour mixture into lined custard cups.
3. Place 4 cupcakes at a time in the oven, spaced about 1 inch apart. (Eight is too many and will not bake properly.)
4. Bake, uncovered, on BAKE for 3 to 3½ minutes.
5. Remove from oven and let stand; allow tops to dry out slightly.
6. Frost as desired.

Sticky Buns

6 servings

⅓ cup dark brown sugar, firmly packed **⅓ cup chopped nuts**
3 tablespoons butter or margarine **1 can (8 ounces) refrigerated biscuits**

1. Combine brown sugar, butter, and 1 tablespoon water in an 8-inch round baking dish.
2. Cook, uncovered, on ROAST for 2 minutes, or until butter melts.
3. Stir mixture and spread over bottom of pan. Sprinkle nuts over top. Place biscuits on top of mixture.
4. Bake, uncovered, on ROAST for 4 to 5 minutes, or until biscuits are firm and no longer doughy.
5. Let stand about 2 minutes. Invert on a flat serving plate.

Apple Pie

7 medium apples
¾ cup sugar
2 tablespoons all-purpose flour
⅛ teaspoon salt
1 teaspoon ground cinnamon

¼ teaspoon ground nutmeg
1 recipe pie crust
1 to 2 teaspoons lemon juice
2 tablespoons butter

1. Pare and slice apples. Mix in a bowl with sugar, flour, salt, cinnamon, and nutmeg. Set aside.
2. Roll out half of the pie crust and fit in the bottom of a 9-inch pie dish. Put apples in pie crust. Sprinkle lemon juice over top if apples are not too tart. Dot with butter. Roll out remainder of pie crust and fit over apples. Seal edges and cut slits in top of pie.
3. Cook on HIGH for 10 minutes, or until apples are tender.
4. While apples are cooking, preheat conventional oven to 450° F.
5. When apples are tender, bake pie in conventional oven 12 to 14 minutes, or until crust is golden brown.
6. Serve warm or cold.

Note: The kind of pie crust that is used makes a difference in the browning time. Packaged pie crust mix browns faster than homemade.

Cherry Cheese Pie

⅓ cup butter or margarine
1¼ cups graham cracker crumbs
¼ cup all-purpose flour
Sugar
1 package (8 ounces) cream cheese, softened

1 egg, lightly beaten
1 cup dairy sour cream, divided
1¾ teaspoons vanilla extract, divided
1 can (21 ounces) prepared cherry pie filling

1. Put butter in a 9-inch pie plate. Melt on ROAST for 2 to 3 minutes.
2. Add graham cracker crumbs, flour, and 4 teaspoons sugar to melted butter in pie plate and blend well. Press mixture evenly over bottom and up sides of pie plate. Set aside.
3. Beat together softened cream cheese and ⅓ cup sugar until well blended. Add egg, ¼ cup sour cream, and ¾ teaspoon vanilla. Beat until light and fluffy. Pour into prepared graham cracker crust.
4. Cook on REHEAT for 4 minutes.
5. Remove from oven and cool 8 minutes on a cooling rack.
6. Beat together ¾ cup sour cream with 2 tablespoons sugar and 1 teaspoon vanilla. Spoon carefully over top of cooked cheese mixture.
7. Cook on REHEAT for 4 minutes, or just until sour cream is set.
8. Spoon cherry pie filling around edge of pie.
9. Chill thoroughly in refrigerator before serving.

FOLLOWING PAGES: Left, *Baked Custard;* right, *Old-Fashioned Indian Pudding;* page 143.

Pecan Pie

1 9-inch pie

¼ cup butter or margarine
⅓ cup brown sugar
1 cup corn syrup
3 eggs, lightly beaten

1 teaspoon vanilla
Pinch of salt
1 cup pecan halves
1 baked 9-inch pastry shell

1. Place butter in a medium-size glass bowl. Cook on HIGH for 1½ minutes, or until butter is melted.
2. Stir in remaining ingredients except pastry shell. Pour mixture into shell.
3. Cook on BAKE for 10 to 12 minutes, or until custard center is set.
4. Cool and serve with whipped cream, if desired.

Pumpkin Pie

1 9-inch pie

2 eggs, lightly beaten
1½ cups solid-pack cooked pumpkin
¾ cup sugar
½ teaspoon salt
1 teaspoon ground cinnamon

½ teaspoon ground ginger
¼ teaspoon ground cloves
1 can (14½ ounces) evaporated milk
1 9-inch baked pastry shell

1. Combine eggs, pumpkin, sugar, salt, and spices and blend well. Stir in milk and make a smooth mixture.
2. Remove ⅔ cup of this mixture and set aside. Pour remaining mixture into baked pastry shell.
3. Cook on SIMMER for 15 minutes. Turn pie and cook on SIMMER for 20 minutes.
4. Let pie stand 20 minutes to continue cooking.
5. Cool before cutting. Serve with flavored whipped cream, since top of pie may have a rough appearance.

Note: Pour reserved pumpkin mixture into custard cups, filling them three-quarters full. Cook on SIMMER for 5 to 6 minutes, or until a knife inserted near the center comes out clean.

Pie Crust

Make up half the recipe of your favorite pie crust or use a mix. Bake a 9-inch shell on HIGH for 3 to 4 minutes. Check pie shell and press it back up if it needs it. Bake on HIGH for 1 minute, or until pie crust is cooked.

Brandied Strawberry Sauce

1½ cups

1 pint fresh strawberries
1 cup sugar
1 tablespoon cornstarch

2 tablespoons lemon juice
2 tablespoons brandy

1. Clean and crush strawberries.

2. Combine sugar and cornstarch in a 1-quart mixing bowl. Stir in lemon juice and crushed strawberries.
3. Cook, covered, on REHEAT about 5 minutes, or until mixture comes to a boil and is clear.
4. Cool slightly. Stir in brandy. Chill well before serving.

Baked Custard   8 small servings

4 eggs	**2 to 2½ cups milk**
¼ cup sugar	**1 teaspoon vanilla extract**
¼ teaspoon salt	**Ground nutmeg**

1. Beat eggs until fluffy. Add sugar and salt and continue beating until thick and lemon-colored. Beat in milk and vanilla.
2. Divide mixture into 8 small custard cups. Sprinkle with nutmeg.
3. Arrange 4 custard cups in an 8-inch square glass baking dish. Fill dish about half full with boiling water. Cook on BAKE for 9 minutes.
4. Remove and let stand 5 minutes. Repeat with remaining 4 cups.

Note: This custard can be baked in an 8-inch cake dish. The consistency will be a little softer. If desired, bake on BAKE for 25 to 30 minutes, or until almost set.

Old-Fashioned Indian Pudding   4 to 6 servings

2 cups milk, divided	**1 egg, beaten**
¼ cup yellow cornmeal	**¼ cup molasses**
2 tablespoons sugar	**1 tablespoon melted butter or**
½ teaspoon salt	**margarine**
½ teaspoon ground cinnamon	**Vanilla ice cream**
¼ teaspoon ground ginger	

1. Pour 1½ cups milk into a 1½-quart casserole. Heat on SIMMER for 5 minutes.
2. Combine cornmeal, sugar, salt, cinnamon, and ginger. Stir into hot milk.
3. Cook, uncovered, on SIMMER for 4 minutes.
4. Beat together egg, molasses, and butter. Stir a small amount of hot milk mixture into egg mixture. Return to casserole. Stir well.
5. Cook, uncovered, on SIMMER for 6 minutes.
6. Pour remaining ½ cup cold milk carefully over top of pudding. Do not stir. Cook, uncovered, on SIMMER for 3 minutes, or until set.
7. Let stand 10 to 15 minutes before serving.
8. Serve warm, topped with vanilla ice cream.

FOLLOWING PAGES: Left, *Baked Apples Supreme*, page 147; *Rhubarb Betty*, page 152.

Vanilla Mousse with Strawberry Sauce

8 to 10 servings

2 envelopes unflavored gelatin

1½ cups sugar, divided

1½ cups milk

2 eggs, separated

1 tablespoon vanilla extract

1 pint heavy cream, whipped

1 pint fresh strawberries

2 tablespoons cornstarch

½ cup lemon juice

2 tablespoons butter

1. Combine gelatin and 1 cup sugar in a mixing bowl and blend well. Stir in milk.
2. Cook, uncovered, on HIGH for 5 minutes, or until hot.
3. Beat egg yolks in a small dish. Gradually stir in a small amount of hot milk mixture. Add to large bowl of hot milk mixture. Blend well.
4. Cook, uncovered, on BAKE for about 4 minutes, or just until bubbles form around edge of bowl. Do not overcook or mixture will curdle.
5. Stir in vanilla. Place bowl in a pan or bowl of ice water. Cool until custard mounds when dropped from a spoon.
6. Beat egg whites until stiff but not dry. Fold into custard mixture. Fold in whipped cream. Turn mixture into a 2-quart mold. Chill in the refrigerator until set.
7. To make the sauce: Clean and hull berries. Reserve 1 cup of the best berries for garnish. Force the remainder through a food mill, or blend in an electric blender. Put through a strainer to remove seeds.
8. Combine the remaining ½ cup sugar with cornstarch in a 1-quart mixing bowl. Gradually stir in 1 cup water.
9. Cook, uncovered, on HIGH for 3 to 4 minutes, or until mixture comes to a boil and is clear.
10. Stir in lemon juice, butter, and strawberry puree. Chill sauce.
11. Unmold mousse on a serving platter. Garnish with whole strawberries. Serve with chilled strawberry sauce.

Packaged Pudding Mix

4 servings

1 package (3¼ ounces) pudding mix, any flavor

2 cups milk

1. Combine pudding mix and milk in a 1-quart bowl or measuring cup. Blend well.
2. Cook, uncovered, on HIGH for 2 minutes. Stir well. Cook, uncovered, on HIGH for 3 to 4 minutes, or until mixture comes to a boil and starts to thicken.
3. Remove from oven and stir well.
4. Pour into serving dishes and cool before serving.

Party-Pretty Pudding

8 servings

2 packages (3¼ ounces each) pudding mix, vanilla flavored

2 pints fresh strawberries, hulled, sliced, and sweetened

1. Prepare pudding according to preceding directions. Cool well.
2. In a pretty glass serving dish, spoon one-third of the cooled pudding. Cover with half the strawberries.
3. Repeat with a second layer of pudding and the remaining strawberries. Spoon the remaining third of the pudding on top of the strawberries. Top with sweetened whipped cream if desired.
4. Chill well before serving.

Note: If desired, the layers may be made in individual serving dishes.

Quick Crème Brûlée   4 servings

1 package (3¼ ounces) pudding mix,   **Brown sugar**
vanilla flavor

1. Prepare pudding mix according to preceding directions. Pour cooked pudding into a flat baking dish. Cool well and chill.
2. Sift a layer of brown sugar, about ⅛ inch thick, over top of pudding, making sure to cover entire top.
3. Place under a hot broiler and broil until sugar melts and bubbles. Watch carefully so that sugar does not burn.

Baked Apples Supreme   6 servings

6 baking apples   **¼ cup brown sugar**
Lemon juice   **2 teaspoons ground cinnamon**
½ cup slivered almonds   **6 teaspoons butter or margarine**
¼ cup raisins

1. Wash apples and remove core, making a generous cavity in each apple. Remove thin circle of peel around cavity and sprinkle with lemon juice.
2. Mix together almonds, raisins, brown sugar, and cinnamon. Fill cavities with mixture and place each apple in a small custard dish. Put 2 tablespoons of water in dish around apple. Dot each apple with 1 teaspoon butter.
3. Cook on HIGH for 6 minutes.
7. Let stand 2 to 3 minutes before serving.

Quick Peach Delight   4 servings

4 large canned peach halves   **4 teaspoons brown sugar**
1¼ teaspoons butter or margarine **Vanilla ice cream**

1. Drain peaches thoroughly. Place in a 1-quart baking dish. Put ¼ teaspoon butter in center of each peach. Sprinkle 1 teaspoon brown sugar on each peach half.
2. Bake, uncovered, on HIGH for 3 minutes, or until piping hot.
3. Serve warm with a small scoop of ice cream in center of each peach half.

FOLLOWING PAGES: Left, *Party-Pretty Pudding, page 146;* right, *Butterscotch Sauce and Fancy Chocolate Sauce, page 152, used on a banana split.*

Quick Applescotch

4 servings

1 can (1 pound) pie-sliced apples
½ package (6 ounces) butterscotch
flavored morsels
1 tablespoon quick-cooking tapioca
½ tablespoon lemon juice
¼ cup all-purpose flour
¼ cup sugar
½ teaspoon ground cinnamon
¼ cup firm butter or margarine

1. Combine apples, butterscotch morsels, and tapioca in a 1-quart casserole. Sprinkle lemon juice over the top.
2. Combine flour, sugar, and cinnamon in a small bowl. Cut in butter with a pastry blender or two knives until mixture resembles cornmeal. Sprinkle over top of apple mixture.
3. Cook, uncovered, on BAKE for 12 minutes, or until piping hot.
4. Serve warm with heavy cream or ice cream, if desired.

Cranberry Apple Crunch

6 servings

1 cup sugar
2 cups chopped cranberries
2 cups chopped apples
1 cup quick-cooking rolled oats
½ cup firmly packed brown sugar
⅓ cup all-purpose flour
½ teaspoon salt
¼ cup butter or margarine
½ cup chopped nuts
Whipped cream

1. Combine sugar, 1 cup water, cranberries, and apples in a buttered 2-quart casserole or baking dish.
2. Cook, covered, on HIGH for 10 minutes.
3. Mix together oats, sugar, flour, and salt. Cut in butter with two knives to make a coarse mixture. Stir in nuts. Sprinkle over top of cranberry mixture.
4. Cook, covered, on HIGH for 5 minutes.
5. Cook, uncovered, on HIGH for 4 minutes, or until apples are done.
6. Let stand 3 to 4 minutes before serving. Serve with whipped cream.

Apple Betty

6 servings

⅓ cup melted butter or margarine
2 cups fresh bread crumbs
6 cups sliced, peeled, and cored
cooking apples
½ cup firmly packed brown sugar
½ teaspoon ground nutmeg
¼ teaspoon ground cinnamon
1 tablespoon grated lemon peel
(optional)
2 tablespoons lemon juice

1. Toss melted butter with bread crumbs. Put one-third of the buttered bread crumbs in a 2-quart casserole.
2. Combine apples with brown sugar, nutmeg, cinnamon, and lemon peel. Put half of the apple mixture on bread crumbs layer. Cover with one-third of the crumbs. Add remaining apples.
3. Combine lemon juice and ¼ cup water. Pour over apples. Top with remaining buttered crumbs.
4. Cook, covered, on REHEAT for 9 minutes.
5. Remove cover and cook on REHEAT for 15 minutes, or until apples are tender.

Stewed Apricots

½ pound dried apricots
1 cup white raisins
Juice of 1 lemon, or 2 tablespoons
    lemon juice

½ cup sugar
1 can (11 ounces) mandarin oranges,
    drained

1. Rinse apricots and raisins in water. Drain.
2. Put apricots and raisins in a 1½-quart casserole. Add 1½ cups water, and cook, uncovered, on HIGH for 5 minutes.
3. Add lemon juice, sugar, and mandarin oranges. Cook on HIGH for 5 minutes. Let stand 2 or 3 minutes before serving.

Baked Maple Bananas

4 servings

2 tablespoons butter or margarine
3 tablespoons maple syrup

4 bananas
Lemon juice

1. Place butter in a medium-size baking dish. Cook on HIGH for 1 minute, or until butter is melted.
2. Add maple syrup and mix.
3. Place peeled bananas in dish and spoon butter mixture over, so that bananas are well coated. Cook on HIGH for 1 minute. Turn bananas. Cook on HIGH for 1½ minutes.
4. Remove from oven and sprinkle with lemon juice.

Honeyed Blueberries

4 to 6 servings

3 cups bran flakes
½ cup honey
¼ cup sugar

1 teaspoon ground cinnamon
½ teaspoon ground nutmeg
2 cups fresh blueberries

1. In a bowl, combine bran flakes, honey, sugar, cinnamon, and nutmeg.
2. Grease an 8-inch square baking dish. Spread half the bran flakes mixture on the bottom. Cover with half the blueberries. Cover blueberries with remaining bran flakes and top with remaining blueberries.
3. Cook, covered, on HIGH for 4 minutes. Serve hot.

Date-Filled Pears

4 servings

4 fresh Bartlett pears
½ cup pitted dates, cut in small pieces
2 tablespoons light brown sugar

3 tablespoons butter or margarine
⅓ cup dry vermouth

1. Cut pears in half. Peel and core. Place in baking dish, cut-side up.
2. Fill pear centers with cut dates. Sprinkle with brown sugar and dot with butter.
3. Pour vermouth over pears and cook, uncovered, on HIGH for 8 minutes, basting once or twice during cooking time. Let stand 2 or 3 minutes.

Fresh Rhubarb Betty

6 to 8 servings

6 cups diced fresh rhubarb
1¼ cups sugar
2½ tablespoons quick-cooking tapioca
1 teaspoon grated lemon peel

1 tablespoon grated orange peel
2¾ cups soft bread cubes
⅓ cup butter or margarine
1 teaspoon vanilla extract

1. Combine rhubarb, sugar, tapioca, lemon peel, and orange peel in a bowl. Set aside.
2. Put bread cubes in a bowl.
3. Place butter in a 1-cup measure. Cook, covered, on HIGH for 45 seconds, or until butter melts.
4. Pour butter over bread cubes; add vanilla and toss lightly.
5. In a 1½-quart casserole make alternate layers of rhubarb and bread-cube mixture, ending with buttered bread cubes.
6. Cook, covered, on HIGH for 5 minutes, or until rhubarb is cooked.
7. Serve warm or chilled.

Butterscotch Sauce

1 cup

½ cup sugar
½ cup firmly packed dark brown sugar
½ cup light cream

1 teaspoon vanilla extract
2 tablespoons butter
⅛ teaspoon salt

1. Combine all ingredients in a 2-cup measuring cup.
2. Cook, uncovered, on ROAST for about 4 minutes, or until sauce is well blended and hot, stirring once.
3. Serve warm over ice cream.

Fancy Chocolate Sauce

2 cups

1 package (12 ounces) semisweet chocolate bits
2 squares (2 ounces) unsweetened chocolate

1 cup heavy cream
3 tablespoons brandy

1. Combine chocolate bits and unsweetened chocolate in a small mixing bowl.
2. Cook, covered, on BAKE for 5 minutes, or just until chocolate melts. Watch carefully during last minute of cooking so that it does not burn.
3. Stir in cream with a wire whisk to make a smooth paste.
4. Cook, covered, on BAKE for 1 to 1½ minutes, or until piping hot.
5. Stir in brandy.
6. Serve hot over vanilla ice cream or cake squares.

OPPOSITE: *The microwave oven heats frozen foods perfectly,* page 154.

Heating Times for Frozen Cooked Foods

Meat Loaf (2 pounds)

Heat on DEFROST for 6 minutes. Turn and heat on DEFROST for 6 minutes. Let stand 5 minutes.

Cooked Chicken (cut in pieces)

Heat 1 to 1½ pounds fried chicken pieces on DEFROST for 8 minutes. Rearrange chicken pieces and heat on DEFROST for 5 minutes.

Spaghetti Sauce (1 pint)

Place plastic container in oven. Heat on DEFROST for 1 to 2 minutes, just long enough to loosen sauce. Place sauce in a 1-quart casserole. Heat on REHEAT for 3 minutes. Stir and heat on REHEAT for 3 minutes. Stir and heat on REHEAT until piping hot.

Cooked Rice (10-ounce package)

Make a slit in top of bag and place in microwave oven. Heat on REHEAT for 8 to 9 minutes, rearranging rice in bag by squeezing bag once during cooking period.

Chili Con Carne (1 quart)

Heat chili in plastic container on DEFROST for 2 minutes to loosen chili. Turn into a 1½-quart container. Cover and heat on REHEAT for 17 minutes, stirring three times during heating time. Let stand 3 minutes before serving.

Vegetables in Butter Sauce (10-ounce package)

Place plastic pouch in a 1-quart casserole. Slit the top. Heat on HIGH for 5 to 6 minutes.

Frozen TV Dinners (2-course, frozen flat)

Remove cover from tray. Cover with plastic wrap. Heat on REHEAT for 8 to 12 minutes, or until hot. Let stand, covered, 2 minutes.

INDEX